JEWISH HEROES OF THE WILD WEST

adapted for young readers by

MARION MAIDENS

from the original

JEWS AMONG THE INDIANS

by

M. L. MARKS

Published for
The American Jewish Historical Society
by
BLOCH PUBLISHING COMPANY, New York

Adaptation © 1997 by Marion Maidens
From the original *Jews among the Indians* © 1992 M.L. Marks, published by Benison Books.

All rights reserved. No part of this book may be reproduced in whole or in any part by any means, including any photographic, mechanical or electronic reproduction, recording or information storage and retrieval systems, without prior written consent of the publishers, except for brief quotations for the purpose of review.

Library of Congress Cataloging-in-Publication Data

Maidens, Marion.
    Jewish heroes of the Wild West / adapted by Marion Maidens from the original Jews among the Indians by M.L. Marks.
       p.   cm.
    ISBN 0-8197-0623-X
    1. Jews -- West (U.S.)--History--Juvenile literature.   2. West (U.S.)--Ethnic relations--Juvenile literature.   I. Marks, Mel. Jews among the Indians.   II. Title.
F696.3.J5M35   1997
978'.004924--dc21
                                                                96-6602
                                                                      CIP
                                                                        AC

Printed in the United States of America

The American Jewish Historical Society wishes to acknowledge a generous grant from Genevieve G. and Justin L. Wyner that makes publication of this work possible. The Society also salutes Marion Maidens for her faith in, and dedication to, this project. Finally, our gratitude is extended to M.L. Marks for generously providing the use of his original work, JEWS AMONG THE INDIANS, Benison Books, 1992.

CONTENTS

ACKNOWLEDGEMENTS vii

INTRODUCTION. ix

THE FIFTIETH MAN 3

THE MAN WHO PAINTED INDIANS 31

UNCLE JULIUS'S LAST WALK. 75

THE UNUSUAL CASE OF DON SOLOMONO 95

ACKNOWLEDGEMENT

My profoundest thanks in undertaking this simplified version of Melvin Marks' JEWS AMONG THE INDIANS go directly to him for his encouragement and never-failing support. After I had reviewed the book for a group at the Jewish Community Center in Tenafly, New Jersey, where it was very warmly received, many people in the area, myself included, wished to have their own copies. It was while placing an order with Benison Books in Chicago that I first spoke with Mr. Marks, to whom I mentioned the idea of a modified edition for young readers, never dreaming that he would invite me to undertake the project. He referred to it as a "spectacular idea." Without his labors, patience, and careful research, a significant portion of Jewish-American history might remain hidden from many of us.

Affectionate thanks also belong to Matthew and David Wolpert, of Demarest, New Jersey, grandsons of my dear friend Beatrice Ginsberg, who provided an attentive audience for the initial effort and whose excited responses clearly justified the plan for a juvenile revision.

Most important in this endeavor is Melinda Beth Maidens, my daughter, whose intellectual curiosity brought the original book to my attention while browsing through the library at the Jewish Center of Teaneck, New Jersey, and who, throughout her life, has constantly proved that "Reading maketh a full man"—in this case, woman. For her lifetime practice of sharing reading experiences with me and for her timely discovering of JEWS AMONG THE INDIANS, the source of my pleasure in producing JEWISH HEROES OF THE WILD WEST, I dedicate this effort to her.

INTRODUCTION

Before Israel became a nation after the War for Independence in 1948, Jews were not really thought of as fighters. More typically, they were type-cast as scholars, doctors, lawyers, teachers, and merchants. The stories in this book, JEWISH HEROES OF THE WILD WEST, will do much toward dispelling such stereotypes by introducing to you another dimension of Jewish life and contributions to our development in America—a dimension in which bravery, imagination, ingenuity as well as native talent and curiosity caused these heroes to risk much in a new land whose destiny they passionately believed in.

Similarly, in a new approach called multi-cultural education, the contribution of many groups to American life is stressed and helps to enrich the traditional curricula we have followed. Such an approach offers endless opportunities for students to learn about themselves in relation to others, as well as working with others to strengthen our society, which we all hold so dear and to which we owe so much.

Jewish students in particular focus largely on the great waves of immigration from Eastern Europe in the late nineteenth and early twentieth centuries as the real beginning of our lives here. Many young people have learned from their family histories of the arrival of great-grandparents and grandparents at Ellis Island, in New York, the famous place of entry for those fleeing the pogroms in Russia, Poland, and Romania. In these violent attacks tens of thousands of men, women, and children were mercilessly slaughtered simply because they were Jewish. We also know that many of those early arrivals settled in and around New York and along the Eastern seaboard to work in what had come to be called "sweatshops" because of the inhumane conditions they were forced to endure. We can rightly say, therefore, that many of our ancestors came here to escape religious persecution or simply to take advantage of economic opportunities in a newly-developing land.

However, from the very beginning of European discovery of America, there were those Jews who, like many others, were plainly adventurers and who had very different reasons for casting their lot in an unknown, possibly dangerous, place. JEWISH HEROES OF THE WILD WEST recounts some of these adventures, largely unknown to most Jewish children.

Our earliest Jewish adventurers were five *Converso** Jews

---

*Note: *Converso*, as the word suggests, in Spanish means one who has converted. However, the Spaniards had another term for those who practiced Judaism in secret—*Marranos*, which means "Swine."

who sailed with Columbus. *Conversos* were those Jews who outwardly became Christians during the Inquisition in Spain in order to spare their lives. Some practiced Judaism and kept their identities in the privacy of their own homes. Among those five were Maistre Bernal, the official doctor for the expedition, and Marco, the surgeon. Another Jew, Luis de Torres, was the interpreter Columbus took with him on his first voyage. As a matter of fact, without the help of Abraham Senior, a Jew, Ferdinand and Isabella of Spain could never have financed Columbus's undertaking at all.

Hernando de Castro, also a Jew who settled in Cuba, introduced to the New World the cultivation of sugar cane which eventually became an important export in the economic life of Cuba and other Caribbean islands.

The work of Levi Ben Gerson, a Jewish astronomer, helped Columbus navigate during his voyage, and astronomical tables drawn up by Judah Ben Moses, Isaac ibn Sid, Abraham Zacuto, and Joseph Vecinho, all Sephardic Jews, were carried and used in that fateful trip to the New World.

Because of the Inquisition which had driven the Jews out of Spain and Portugal, many who refused to convert took refuge in South America, where Pizarro had explored early in the sixteenth century. Sadly, the long arm of the Inquisition searched out these escapees and they had to flee again, this time to the safety of New Amsterdam, the first Dutch colony in North America, later to become New York when the British conquered it.

About that time, one Jacob Bar Simson earned the distinction of being an early Jewish adventurer, for he had the courage to go where no other Jew had ever been. In 1654, he left Brazil for the Dutch colony of New Amsterdam (now New York) where the first Jewish community in America had been established. Following him came a group of fellow Jews, also from Brazil, although they had originally come from Holland where they were welcomed after fleeing the Inquisition. On the way, the travelers had been robbed and therefore could not pay their passage money to the captain of the ship on which they had sailed. As a result, two of the passengers were held hostage until their belongings could be sold to pay their debt.

Another Jewish adventurer of a different kind was Jacob Lumbrozo, one of the first doctors to practice medicine in America. He settled in Maryland in 1656. Not being able to earn enough as a doctor, he was obliged to trade with the local Indians to make ends meet.

Although the first congregation in America was established in New York in 1703 (Shearith Israel, which still exists), it was not until 1728 that public Jewish worship could be held. In general, Jews were not welcome newcomers in America, with the exception of Rhode Island, where Roger Williams, the first governor, founded the colony on the unwavering principle of religious tolerance and freedom. His beautiful example paved the way for our cherished First Amendment, which grants religious freedom to all. The synagogue in Newport, Rhode Island, Jeshuath Israel, dedicated in 1763, has been declared a national shrine. Henry Wadsworth Longfellow, our great nineteenth-century poet, composed a moving and sensitive tribute to the first Jewish settlers buried in the synagogue graveyard. It is appropriately called "The Jewish Cemetery at Newport."

In the years before the Revolution, many Jews distinguished themselves in new and effective ways, often leaving fairly secure lives in Europe to emigrate to The New World. One such adventurer was Moses Levy, who left a thriving business in London to become a ship owner in New York in 1705. There he became leader of the small but growing Jewish community.

Because Jews have traditionally maintained ideals of human liberty and equality which they themselves had so often been denied, most became firm supporters of our Revolution. Even those with modest means helped raise money for food, supplies and armaments when the time came. They also served in every Colonial militia during the War for Independence. Because there were 26 Jews from South Carolina alone under Colonel Washington, their troop became known as "The Jews' Company," taking part in the battle of Beaufort under General Moultrie.

In Philadelphia, Haym Salomon, a Polish immigrant who arrived in America only four years before the war began, helped to finance the Revolution and died bankrupt because of his devotion to the American nation, while one Isaac Moses almost ruined his family finances by providing three thousand pounds to buy food for the starving troops of the Continental Army.

There was a Jewish governor of Georgia shortly after the Revolution in 1801. David Emanuel's bravery during the siege of Savannah caused the largest county in the state to be named Emanuel County in his honor.

The Civil War (1861-1865) also produced its share of Jewish participants. Our nation was torn apart by differences over the slavery issue. Judah Benjamin, a brilliant and successful lawyer who was aptly called "the brains of the Confederacy," was elected United States Senator from Louisiana twice—in 1853 and in 1859.

Jewish Heroes of the Wild West

Always known for their skill in medical matters, Jews produced a Union hero in the form of Lt. Col. Israel Moses, whose new treatment for gunshot wounds saved many lives in the Civil War. His work remains part of the medical annals of Mount Sinai Hospital in New York, one of the world's foremost teaching hospitals.

There was even a chaplain for Northern Jewish soldiers during the Civil War. Although Michael M. Allen had never been ordained, he was allowed to act in place of an ordained rabbi because there were so many Jewish soldiers in the Cameron Dragoons, who were mounted soldiers with heavy arms. A special act of Congress had to be passed in order for Allen to perform his duties, since he was not a Christian. Finally, in 1862, that limitation was eliminated so he could care for the spiritual needs of his Jewish comrades.

In modern America, we Jews may be justifiably proud of our contributions in various fields. Older relatives in your family may well tell their recollections of being refused admission to certain schools or colleges. Those who became exceptions were adventurous enough to pioneer in seeking the best possible education in spite of the isolation or bigotry they may have experienced from their classmates, and some of the most outstanding figures of the twentieth century in music, the fine arts, industry, commerce, literature, and government have been Jews who, in earlier years, persisted in their efforts against deeply-held prejudices to achieve recognition. We may indeed be grateful for the dignity and fame those "adventurers" brought to us, despite our minority status in this country as well as the world, to which we have given nearly forty per cent of Nobel Prize winners in literature as well as various branches of medicine and science.

But now, read with pleasure the exploits of Jews in the West, to whom we owe so much, but above all, remembrance and thankfulness.

Teaneck, New Jersey
February, 1997

THE FIFTIETH MAN

Sigmund Schlesinger, hero of the Battle of Beecher Island
American Jewish Archives

Jewish Heroes of the Wild West

THE FIFTIETH MAN

It was a day the two small Shlesinger children would never forget. It had been a warm afternoon in Cleveland, Ohio, and their father had taken them to see Buffalo Bill's Wild West Show. Buffalo Bill had been the greatest of the Pony Express riders and buffalo hunters. He also had with him Annie Oakley, the famous rifle shot. There were cowboys—racing, lassoing wild horses, and riding bucking broncos. There were also musical military drills and amazing feats of horsemanship by soldiers of the Sixth United States Cavalry.

Of course, there were Indians doing war dances in full headdress or racing on their western bronco ponies. There were Indians with war paint on their faces, attacking the Deadwood Mail Coach and being pushed back by Buffalo Bill and the cowboys, or Indians attacking a wagon train crossing the plains and again being turned back by Buffalo Bill and the cowboys.

Never had Lillian and her brother Louis seen anything like that! The battles between the cowboys and the Indians excited them most, however, for their father, Sigmund, told them bedtime stories about that same Buffalo Bill, Wild Bill

Jewish Heroes of the Wild West

Hickok, and General Forsyth who all took part in battles with Indians on the plains.

How these stories thrilled the two children! The best part was having seen with their own eyes the performances based on their father's stories. When the action was over, the father introduced his children to Buffalo Bill and the cowboys in the tent they used as a dressing-room. The children watched their father and the tall buffalo hunter with his long, flowing white hair and beard hug each other after they had shaken hands.

Father then took the children to the Indians' tent. Some of them had fought white settlers thirty years earlier on the plains of Kansas and Colorado, but now the children were happy to see that their father and the Indians were friends.

The year that Buffalo Bill came to Cleveland was 1897, and the children's father, Sigmund Shlesinger, who talked so easily with the great buffalo hunter and the Indians, was then in his forties.

A quiet man, he had, in his own way, become an important member of the Cleveland Jewish community. A tobacco wholesaler, he gave his time and money generously through many charitable groups to which he belonged: the Hungarian

Aid Society, B'nai Brith and the Knights of Pythias, a Jewish fraternal organization. He was vice-president of his temple and had also helped to organize the Cleveland Relief Society, the Hebrew Free Loan Association, the Educational Alliance, and the Federation of Jewish Charities. He worked tirelessly to help those less fortunate than himself.

To General A. Forsyth and a small band of Indian scouts, Sigmund Shlesinger—or Slinger—as they called him then—was a hero of one of the most violent Indian battles ever to occur on the western plains—the battle, September 17, 1868, on the Arickaree Fork of the Republican River, just west of the Kansas line and seventeen miles below Wray, in Yuma County, Colorado.

It took place between a band of fifty Indian scouts commanded by Forsyth (who was then still a colonel) and an army of Cheyenne, Oglala Sioux, Arapahos, Kiowas, and Comanches, led by the great Cheyenne warrior, Chief Roman Nose. There were over 1,000 Indians!

The battle on the Arickaree Fork was later called the Battle of Beecher Island in memory of Lieutenant Frederick Beecher because it was during that fierce assault on the scouts that Lieutenant Beecher of the Third United States Infantry was killed.

This was a very important battle because it helped stop tribes from warring against each other and eventually helped them accept the idea of living on reservations.

Forsyth hoped that the fighting would not be in vain, that the day would come when the Indians would accept the white settlers and the "Iron Horse" (railroad) which had become an important part of the white man's world.

Shlesinger's story began with his arrival in America from Hungary in 1864, when he was just fourteen years old. The Civil War was coming to an end then, and his main concern was how to earn a living in New York. He could not then imagine in his wildest dreams that he would ever come face to face with Indians, let alone be pinned down under siege for nine days by over 1,000 of them!

But fate had an interesting future planned for the young man. From his home in New York, where he had a job as horsecar conductor, he was hired as a clerk by a businessman in Leavenworth, Kansas, and that was when he took his first step toward meeting with Chief Roman Nose.

Shlesinger stayed on his job in Leavenworth for about a year before becoming restless because his work was dull and he

Artist R.F. Zogbaum's depiction of Sigmund Shlesinger and Colonel George Forsyth at the Battle of Beecher Island, 1868.
American Jewish Archives

wanted to explore other communities in Kansas where he might earn more money and look for new adventures.

He went first to Johnson City (Fort Riley, Kansas) which was then the farthest point the Union Pacific railroad tracks had reached. He kept on moving along the route of the railroad, for he had heard that he could make money trading with the railroad workers as well as with the army troops assigned to guard the workers. As new track was laid, new communities sprang up almost overnight along the roadbed, and these bustling new towns offered many business opportunities.

Shlesinger had many temporary jobs: clothing store clerk, bartender, cook, waiter, mule herder and shoveler for the railroad. It was during his work in railroad construction that he met Buffalo Bill and Wild Bill Hickok. He really admired both of these men, and in his later years he described Hickok as being "one of the finest gentlemen I had met on the plains."

In the summer of 1868, Shlesinger fell on hard times. There was nowhere to turn for help because he had no family connections in this strange part of the world. Out of money and hungry, he went from army camp to army camp in search of work. During this time, he learned that Colonel George

Forsyth, at Fort Hays, Kansas, was pulling together a company of experienced frontiersmen to serve as scouts against the Indians.

The Indian problem had become serious. With the building of the Union Pacific railroad after the Civil War, relations between the white settlers and the Indians had become strained to the breaking point. The Indians destroyed sections of the railroad and tried to chase away the white settlers.

They attacked small communities, killing the men and terrorizing the women and children. To add to the problem, Indians had learned to use firearms during the Civil War and had become quite skilled in using them. As a result, the army came to believe that the Indians had now become dreaded enemies who had to be overcome.

Major General Philip Sheridan, in command of the Department of the Missouri at Fort Harker, Kansas, decided that Indian scouts should immediately be sent out to look for and beat the Indian enemies. This was exactly what Colonel Forsyth had hoped for, and he quickly volunteered to head the command.

In August, 1868, Forsyth received the following orders from the Department of the Missouri:

> Colonel, the general commanding directs that you, without delay, employ fifty (50) first-class, hardy frontiersmen to be used as scouts against the hostile Indians, to be commanded by yourself, with Lieutenant Beecher, Third Infantry, your subordinate. You can enter into such articles of agreement with these men as will compel obedience.
>
> I am, sir, very respectfully, your obedient servant. (Signed) Colonel J. Schyler Crosby, Acting Adjutant General.

Although Forsyth's knowledge of the Indians was limited, this is how he described them. His description reflects his image of them.

> First, that they were shrewd, crafty, treacherous and brave. Secondly, that they were able warriors in that they took no unnecessary risks, attacked generally from ambush and never in an open field unless in overwhelming numbers. Thirdly, that they were savages in all that word implies, gave no quarter, and defeat at their hands meant annihilation, either in the field, or by torture at the stake.

General Sheridan wanted Forsyth to get started as quickly as possible, so he wasted no time in getting a group together—thirty scouts from Fort Harker and another nineteen from Fort Hays. All these men were tough, experienced Indian fighters, some of whom had fought in the Civil War and settled in the West.

Jewish Heroes of the Wild West

By the time Shlesinger appeared at Fort Hays to answer the call for scouts, the group was ready to march. He was taken on in spite of some doubts about his ability because they needed a fiftieth man to complete the party.

General James B. Fry, who was also a historian, gave this account of Colonel Forsyth's reaction to Shlesinger:

> Shlesinger seemed to be inferior, in all respects unfit for service; a Jew, small with narrow shoulders, sunken chest, quiet manner and pipey voice, and little knowledge of firearms or horsemanship; he was indeed unpromising as a son of Mars, and after forty-nine scouts had been obtained, was accepted only that he might be counted on the rolls to make up the fifty, and thus enable the expedition to start. (Note: Mars is the Roman god of war.)

Only five days after Forsyth had received his orders, the scouts were perfectly organized and outfitted. Each man had a Spencer repeating rifle, a Colt revolver, 140 rounds of rifle ammunition, and thirty pounds of revolver ammunition. Each man carried seven days' worth of cooked food in his knapsack.

On August 29, Sheridan ordered Forsyth and his men to move across the Solomon River to Beaver Creek. Then they followed the creek northwest to Fort Wallace, Kansas. Thus they left civilization behind.

Jewish Heroes of the Wild West

During the first day's ride, Shlesinger had many problems. First, he was not used to a horse and saddle so that his bottom became chafed and sore. He had to shift his equipment often and his arm was cramped. Every muscle in his body ached.

When the party made camp the first night, he was exhausted but could get no sleep because he was immediately chosen for guard duty. Nevertheless, with each passing day on the trail, the young man from Hungary became more accustomed to riding horseback, and by the time the party of scouts reached Fort Wallace eight days later, Shlesinger had become a seasoned horseman.

Shlesinger was not well-accepted by most of his comrades. Inexperienced, young, slight of build and being Jewish made them either ignore him or, worse still, make fun of him. Like many Jews before him in a similar situation, he disregarded the hostile treatment he received and did the best job he was capable of in carrying out his duties. Jack Stillwell and Jack Peate, two young scouts about Shlesinger's age, however, were warm and friendly.

At Fort Wallace, Forsyth received word that the Indians were on the warpath. They had attacked a freight train near the fort, leaving two men dead. The scouts assembled quickly and rode after the Indians, but the next day they lost the trail. In spite of this setback, they continued on and a few days later picked up the trail of a few Indian horses, thanks to the head scout, Sharp Glover, who was himself an Indian. Although the trail became wider as they went on and appeared well-trampled with hoof-tracks, still there was no Indian in sight.

Continuing their traveling, the scouts noticed that the hoof-tracks had suddenly appeared further apart. This suggested that riders were leaving the main body of their group along the way. The Indian scout Glover was able to conclude that the scouts had been seen by the Indian warriors who were aware that they were being followed. From hiding places along the trail, the scouts' every move was being watched.

By now the trail was growing narrower and narrower. They were finally led into the middle fork of the Republican River, the Arickaree Fork. It was too quiet for comfort, but Forsyth, in spite of his fears, was determined to confront any war party, no matter how much the scouts would be outnumbered.

On the evening of September 16, the scouts camped on the grassy banks of the river in a large meadow which sloped gently down to the edge of the water. Close to the bank was a small, sandy island; this was a sandbar. On the scouts' opposite flank was a hill overlooking the meadow where they camped.

After their horses were tied down and guards posted, the scouts ate a little of their small remaining food supply and bedded down for the night. They had come about 150 miles since leaving Fort Wallace, but even though they were weary they could not sleep easily. There was something frightening in the night stillness, and the suspicious absence of the Indian warriors from the time they had left the fort made them feel they were facing real dangers. In that Colorado darkness, each scout could feel the Indians close by.

Their fears were proved right. As dawn broke on September 17, Shlesinger was awakened by someone shouting, "Indians!" He felt his head swimming with the fear of sudden death. About a dozen Indians were stampeding the scouts' horses! Moments later, he looked up and saw in the distance an army of Indians, over 1,000 of them, thundering down at him, their ponies in full gallop, their lances decorated with brightly-colored streamers.

Now they came closer, rifle fire coming from all directions. Shlesinger heard Colonel Forsyth desperately give the command to fall back to the sandbar. Scrambling furiously, the scouts clawed their way onto the sandy island while the colonel barked directions for them to take up battle positions. In the sand, the scouts tried frantically to make pits deep enough to protect them.

Suddenly Shlesinger heard the colonel cry out in pain. He had received a bullet wound in the left knee and another one in his right thigh. Meanwhile, the attack continued for what seemed like hours, but in reality it was over very quickly. With shaking hands, the young Shlesinger had managed to fire off several rounds at the attacking Indians! He was truly surprised to find how calm he could be when the crisis finally came.

The Indians now withdrew from this first assault in order to prepare for another charge. During the attack, the scouts received many injuries. Lieutenant Beecher was killed, and the acting surgeon (the scouts' doctor) J. H. Moors was shot in the head. Three days later he died of his wound. In spite of losing all the scouts' horses, in spite of the wounds of his men, and in spite of the wounds in both his legs, Forsyth was still able to command.

Later in the morning, as the scouts had expected, the Indians returned. By then, the shock of the first attack had worn off, and Shlesinger and his comrades were able to shoot at the Indians, holding them off from their shelter in the sand pits they had dug. These sharpshooters had been trained very carefully for just such events.

From his pit, Shlesinger saw the Indian leader, Chief Roman Nose, the great Cheyenne fighter, a huge man on a magnificent chestnut horse. He was naked except for a bright sash around his waist, the moccasins on his feet, and a dazzingly-bright war bonnet. His face was streaked with war paint, and as he rode shouting encouragement to his warriors, he made fun of the scouts while staring death in the face.

Suddenly, the great chief's horse reared, and the mighty Roman Nose went down, the victim of a scout's bullet!

Sharp Glover, the Indian scout with the party, identified the warriors as Northern Cheyenne, Oglala, and Sioux, along with a number of other tribes. Roman Nose was in command of all the tribes, but there were other tribal chiefs as well—Big Mouth, Tall Bull, Yellow Bear, Minnimmuck, and Little Robe. After Roman Nose was killed, Minnimmuck, a younger chief, took over the command.

By nightfall of September 17, the scouts realized how much trouble they were in. They were so heavily outnumbered that their mission seemed hopeless. Colonel Forsyth, by then in great pain from his wounds, asked for volunteers to return to Fort Wallace for help, for that would be their only chance for survival. Shlesinger's friend, Jack Stillwell, was first to volunteer. He chose an older scout, Pierre Trudeau, to be his partner, and the two set out on foot for Fort Wallace on the night of September 17.

Artist Byron E. Wolfe's depiction of the charge of Chief Roman Nose at the Battle of Beecher Island, 1868.
American Jewish Archives

The following day, the Indians attacked again, but Forsyth's men hung on and forced them back. Although they did not receive many wounds this time, all their food was gone and their ammunition was running low. The scouts also feared that their comrades would not make it safely to Fort Wallace, so Forsyth, growing weaker and weaker, two days later decided to send two more scouts to the fort. Unfortunately, they were spotted by the Indians and had to return. Now all their hopes for rescue depended on Stillwell and Trudeau.

By September 22, even though the weary scouts had managed to keep the Indians away after repeated attacks, they gave up all hope. They were hungry, thirsty, disorganized and discouraged. In the attempt to ease their hunger, they even tried boiling the carcasses of their dead horses. They salted the meat with gunpowder to try to make it edible, but this did not work. The meat could not be eaten. All they could do was lie in their shelter pits, half-asleep, too weak to offer any resistance. Forsyth was now running a high fever and was too sick to encourage his troops, but the Indians were having the same difficulties. With their great leader, Roman Nose, dead, the power he had to keep the tribes together was gone, and so the Indians too lost their fighting spirit. Each following attack was less deadly than the one before.

In the meantime, traveling only at night, Stillwell and Trudeau arrived at Fort Wallace. They had managed to get to Cheyenne Wells, the stage coach station, about thirty miles from the fort. From there they were able to ride the stage to the fort. It had taken them five days, and during their journey they managed to get past several parties of Indians.

Good things began to happen for the scouts from that point on. Three days after Stillwell and Trudeau reached Fort Wallace, a troop of the Tenth Cavalry under Colonel L. H. Carpenter rescued the scouts. Even though the Indians had spotted the Carpenter relief party before Colonel Forsyth, they were too weak and scattered to offer resistance.

The battle on the Arickaree Fork was over!

The bedraggled scouts had survived nine days of a bitter siege. Five were killed, sixteen were wounded, but Colonel Forsyth recovered from his wounds. It took him two years.

Among these brave scouts there was one coward, Whalen. The Colonel made the following comparison between Whalen and Shlesinger:

> Only one man in my command had failed me...he had joined the command at Fort Hayes, and I was much impressed by his appearance. No one seemed to know

him as he was a recent arrival at the post...tall, well-built, brown hair and black eyes, a flowing beard midway to his waist, well-mounted on his own horse, a good rider and with a pleasing address, he not only impressed me favorably but others as well. On our first scout from Fort Hayes to Fort Wallace he spoke of several Indian engagements in the far north in which he had taken part, and so won upon me by his statements and general bearing that I thought him, for this especial service, quite invaluable. Something of a joker, he was inclined to guy and poke fun at some of the odd characters of the command and especially at a young Jew of about 19 or 20 who had enrolled just at the last moment at Fort Hayes to complete the complement of 50 men.

He was a short...rather awkward and boyish young fellow with cherry cheeks and verdant in some ways, and entirely new to campaigning, but I soon noticed his good care of his horse, his strict obedience to orders, and his evident anxiety to learn his duty and do it. Furthermore, my experience with men of his race during the Civil War, with a single exception, had strongly impressed me in their favor as being brave men and good soldiers. Imagine my surprise and astonishment, therefore, to discover that my fine looking scout was an absolute failure and coward, while as for the little Jew...! Well, the Indian that from dawn to dusk was incautious enough to expose any part of his person within the range of his rifle had no cause to complain of a want of marked attention on the part of that brave and active young Israelite...in fact, he most worthily proved himself a gallant soldier among brave men.

In addition to praising Shlesinger for his bravery under fire, he also gave him credit for killing a coyote which served as emergency food for the pinned-down scouts.

Shlesinger kept a diary which did not come to public light until 1951. His daughter Lillian had kept it. While this diary did not add anything to the published accounts of the battle, it did provide readers with a fine understanding of the simple courage of a young immigrant Jew. The diary covers the period from August 28 to September 22, 1868, and it is written in a little notebook only three and a half by eight inches. The events are written down clearly, but with many misspellings, for which we must surely forgive Shlesinger, who was not that fluent in English.

September 16: Seen signal fire on Hill 3 miles off in evening late.

September 17: About 12 Indians carched on us stampeedet 7 horse. 10 minute after about 600 Indians attacket us. Kilt Beecher, Culver and Wilson. Woundet 19 Man and Kilt all the horses. We was without Grubb and water all day. Dug holes in the sand with our hands.

September 18: In the night I dug my hole deeper. Cut off meat of the horses and hung it up on bushes. Indians made a charge at us at Day Brake but retreatet. Kept Shooting nearly all day they put up a White Flag. Left us at 9 O'Clock in the evening. Rained all night.

A page from the battlefield diary of Sigmund Schlesinger.
American Jewish Archives

September 19: The Indians came back again. Kept sharp-shooting all day. Two boys startet for Fort Wallace. Rained all night.

September 20: Dr. Moore died last night. Raining part of the Day. Snow about 1 inches thick. Indians kept sharpshooting.

September 21: Scalpt 3 Indians which were found about 15 feet from my hole concealt in grass.

September 22: Kilt a Coyote and eat him all up.

Shortly after the scouts were rescued, Shlesinger resigned from the command and returned to New York. He told his friends about his adventures but nobody believed him. Even when he showed them some of his battle souvenirs including a bloodstained blanket, they were still not convinced. In fact, one friend even asked him, "How much did they (the souvenirs) cost?" Two years later, when he moved to Cleveland, his stories of the battle continued to be met with disbelief, for there was no evidence to prove his story was true.

The time finally came when he would receive credit for his role in the Battle of Beecher Island. In August, 1893, twenty-five years later, General Fry wrote an article. Once and for all time, it put an end to the doubts about Shlesinger's adventures, for the article contained a poem honoring the young scout:

"When the foe charged on the breastworks,
With madness and despair,
And the bravest souls were tested,
The little Jew was there.

When the weary dozed on duty
And the wounded needed care,
When another shot was called for,
The little Jew was there.

With the festering dead around them,
Shedding poison in the air,
When the crippled chieftan ordered,
the little Jew was there."

In 1895, General Forsyth (originally the colonel who had been promoted) published his version of the battle in HARPER'S MAGAZINE. It contained the names of all those who had taken part and it gave Shlesinger the recognition he deserved.

Two years later, Forsyth received a letter from Rabbi Henry Cohen of Galveston, Texas, regarding Shlesinger. The general by then was living in Wilkes-Barre, Pennsylvania, and this is the letter he wrote in answer to Rabbi Cohen:

My dear Rabbi Cohen:
In answer to your inquiry of December 7, regarding Mr. Sigmund Shlesinger, who served in my command on the Western frontier in 1867-68, and who was with me in my fight with the Sioux Indians in the Arickaree

Fork, I have a high admiration of the courage and splendid pluck and endurance of young Shlesinger on the occasion mentioned...

He had never been in action prior to our fight with the Indians and throughout the whole engagement which was one of the hardest, if not the very hardest, ever fought on the Western plains, he behaved with great courage, cool persistence and a dogged determination that won my unstinted admiration as well as that of his comrades, many of whom had seen service throughout the War of Rebellion on one side or the other.

I can accord him no higher praise than that he was the equal in manly courage, steady and persistent devotion to duty and unswerving and tenacious pluck of any man in my command.

It is a real pleasure to state this fact. I especially mention the pluck and endurance of this young son of Israel and speak of him as a worthy descendant of King David.

> I am, sir, with sincere respect,
> Very truly yours,
> George A. Forsyth
> General, U.S. Army

In the years that followed, Shlesinger exchanged letters with many of his comrades. Some even came to Cleveland to visit him, and he also traveled around the country to visit them. The scouts had formed a bond that was quite touching, and their feelings for each other added to all they had been through together gave them the idea to form the Beecher Island Battle Memorial Association to keep alive the memory of the little band of scouts who fought so nobly for their country.

About 1910, Shlesinger, then in his sixties, wrote to the association, describing his friendship with Jack Stillwell:

> Jack and I were the only boys in the company and naturally gravitated toward each other. We were friends as soon as we met and chums before we knew each others' names. When Stillwell finally returned not long after the Carpenter rescue party arrived...Jack jumped from his horse and in his joy to see so many of us alive ...permitted his tears free flow down his good honest cheeks. I kept up correspondence with him all these past years. Last year, he died. He was a big-hearted, jovial fellow, brave to a fault.

He also wrote about Jack Peate.

> One day a man came to my office asking for Sig Shlesinger, and introducing himself as J. J. Peate...You who have met Jack do not need to be told who and what Jack is. You know him to be the personification of all that is generous, kind and noble in a man, exceeded only by his better half. But to me, who had been hungering for a material manifestation of that cherished dream of long ago—to me, who had been longing to meet a comrade, face to face, he was almost an apparition. He was the first man connected with Forsyth's

Jewish Heroes of the Wild West

> scouts to shake my hand in a grip of fellowship. It thrilled my whole being, and I am happy to be counted among his friends to this day, and I hope I always will be...

Continuing his letter to his comrades, Shlesinger wrote:

> Father time exacts his toll. Our years make us susceptible to the inevitable, and when the last one will have answered the eternal call, I would love to believe that kindred souls may resume that cohesive existence of which this world may be the prelude.

These were the closing words of his letter:

> I expect to pass through the world but once; if, therefore, there be any kindness that I can show or any good thing that I can do, let me do it now for I shall not pass this way again.

Sigmund Shlesinger, one Jew among 1,000 Indians, died in April, 1928, at the age of 79. The leaders of the Cleveland Jewish Community came to pay their respects to the man who had worked so hard for so many Jewish causes. Rabbi Abba Hillel Silver, who conducted the services, paid tribute to Shlesinger, praising him for his leadership in many charitable activities.

The Board of Trustees of the temple, in a resolution, saluted him as a fifty-year member "who labored in every cause." His widow, Fannie, and his three children mourned the loss of a good husband and father.

We can imagine that his two older children, Lillian and Louis, were day-dreaming while the rabbi spoke, about that day, so many years before, the never-to-be-forgotten day, when Buffalo Bill came to town and they sat in a special box seat with their father to watch the battles between cowboys and Indians being acted out.

There was one mourner who was a stranger to the Jews of Cleveland. He plainly looked out of place among them. He was a bent, gray-haired old man who had traveled all the way from his home in Beverly, Kansas, to say a last good-bye to a good friend and fallen comrade. He was alone now, this old man, the last surviving member of the little band of scouts who fought so bravely on the Arickaree Fork. His name was Jack Peate, one of the two Jacks who became Shlesinger's devoted friends, who did not make fun of his lack of experience, his foreign accent, and his beginning troubles on horseback. Neither did they ignore him because he was a Jew.

THE MAN WHO PAINTED INDIANS

Solomon Carvalho, Self-Portrait. Barbados, 1844.
American Jewish Archives

THE MAN WHO PAINTED INDIANS

It was the winter of 1853. A man sat huddled in his buffalo robes in the mountains of eastern Utah, trying to warm himself in the sub-zero cold and heavy snow.

He would soon leave the snow bank which gave him his only protection from the storm and begin rounding up the horses which had strayed a mile deeper into the mountains. As he trudged after them, knee-deep in the snow, he found himself thinking of his mother. As a boy in Charleston, South Carolina, he had heard her answer when he asked if he could go out to play one night in bad weather: "I would not allow a cat to go out in such weather, much less my son," his mother had said.

Looking around him, he wrote in his diary, "Dear Soul: How her heart would have ached for me if she had known a hundredth part of my sufferings."

The wilderness of eastern Utah in the dead of winter was a strange place to find Solomon Nunes Carvalho. He was a handsome man, still in his thirties, with long flowing hair. He was something of a momma's boy, very fussy and accustomed to luxuries. Highly educated and fluent in Latin and Greek, he had a very elegant way about him, like that of an aristocrat. In fact, he was an aristocrat among Jews, a grandee, the name given to those Jews of Sephardic descent who first came to the New World.

Yet now he found himself with ten Delaware Indians and several untrustworthy muleskinners as companions. Were it not for Colonel John Charles Frémont, his leader, and Frémont's group of officers—Egloffstein, Fuller, and Strobel—he would have found the Frémont expedition over the Rockies unbearable.

Carvalho first became part of the Frémont expedition one hot August afternoon in 1853. Frémont had come to Charleston to invite Carvalho to accompany him as official artist and daguerreotypist (the earliest form of photography) for his fifth expedition, an exploratory mission through the Rocky Mountains to find a route across the continent which could be used all year 'round by a railroad. Carvalho had jumped at the offer.

But now, in the cold wilderness of Utah, Carvalho, thinking about that August afternoon, wished he had said no. He wrote in his diary, "I should have replied there were no inducements sufficiently powerful to have tempted me." But he had accepted the offer on the spur of the moment, not even stopping to discuss it with his family because he was so delighted at being asked by Frémont, a national hero, to accompany him. It had made no difference at the time that the exploration party would cross fearsome territory which, until then, had been seen only by a few white men, in a part of the country where the winter weather was almost always brutal. Caravalho had high regard for Frémont. He wrote, "I know of no other man to whom I would have trusted my life under similar circumstances."

These details and countless others are carefully described in Carvalho's book, INCIDENTS OF TRAVEL AND ADVENTURE IN THE FAR WEST WITH COLONEL FREMONT'S LAST EXPEDITION, an exciting but sometimes heart-rending account of his experiences with the expedition.

Solomon Carvalho was talented and accomplished. He was, above all things, an artist, one of the first Jews in America to earn his living in that profession. His portraits of some of the great leaders of his time—Lincoln, Brigham Young, Frémont, and Walkara, the Ute Indian chief—are regarded today as priceless works of art. He was also a skilled daguerreotypist, a master of photography, who had been taught by Samuel F. B. Morse himself, the pioneer of that art.

In addition, Carvalho was a teacher, an inventor, an adventurer, a writer, a prayer-book salesman, as well as a deeply religious Jew who helped to found the first Portuguese synagogue in Baltimore. As a man, he was flashy and conceited, and sought the company of famous people. However, this man of Jewish nobility, whose ancestors could be traced back to the 1400's, the time of the Spanish Inquisition, was at heart courageous and tough-minded whose choice it was to undergo some astonishing experiences in his travels through the Rockies with Frémont.

John Charles Frémont crossed and re-crossed great expanses of the Trans-Mississippi West in five expeditions between 1842 and 1853. He followed trails to Oregon and California that had been carved out only by Indians and mountain men. His reports and maps cleared the way for settlers to move westward with some measure of safety. He mapped out trails, established the best times and methods for travel, and pinpointed the location of water holes and grass for livestock grazing. In short, Frémont was advance man for the great western migrations. As his wife, Jessie Benton Frémont, put it, "From the ashes of his campfires have sprung cities."

Despite all his enterprise, Frémont was unable to get government approval for his fifth expedition and had to finance it himself. His first three expeditions had been enormously successful, and he had been hailed as a national hero. His fourth expedition, however, was a disaster. He lost thirteen of his thirty-three men, and there were rumors that one of the thirteen had been killed and eaten by his comrades. To some extent, the failure of the fourth expedition was responsible for the government's denying him support for the fifth expedition. But a more important reason for that failure was the opposition of Jefferson Davis, Secretary of War under President Pierce, and the man responsible for such appointments. No two men were more at odds, both in politics and in the way they thought, than Frémont and Davis. There was scarcely a matter on which they could agree. Most importantly, Davis was pro-slavery and Frémont was an abolitionist. It was because they disagreed on this vital subject that Frémont was denied official support for the expedition.

Two other expeditions were already in the field when Frémont's began. All three were seeking the best railroad route through the Rockies. One expedition was led by Guinn Harris Heap, the other was led by Captain John W. Gunnison. It was the second of these, sponsored by the U.S. Government, that Frémont had hoped to lead. Always strong-willed and

John Charles Frémont. Portrait by Solomon Carvalho c. 1856.
*Courtesy of the Museum of American Art of the
Pennsylvania Academy of Fine Arts, Philadelphia*

independent, Frémont believed that the other two would prove useless, for they were being undertaken in the summer, a season when the railroad would have less trouble crossing the San Juan Mountains, a difficult range to cross in any season, and one that would present impossible problems in the winter. Without a winter survey, the other two expeditions would prove nothing, thought Frémont.

When Carvalho joined the Frémont party, his aristocratic family opposed his putting his life in the hands of a man like Frémont, who was born out of wedlock, a "mountaineer," an "adventurer," and "a man of no education." But Carvalho saw Frémont in a different light—as a man of "high literary attainments," "great mental capacity," and "solid scientific knowledgements," a "man of education," a "man of genius and a gentleman"—"reserved almost to taciturnity (of few words) yet perfectly amiable withal."

Jewish Heroes of the Wild West

Frémont enthusiastically began making preparations for his expedition, buying surveying instruments and field equipment, hiring the men to fill key positions on the expedition. With Carvalho on board, the question of who was going to operate the complicated daguerreotype equipment was evidently answered. At all costs, Frémont wanted to be the first explorer to have a complete photographic record of an expedition. It had been his search for a competent daguerreotypist that led him to Carvalho.

Within a few weeks after being hired by Frémont, Carvalho set out for St. Louis, carrying his painting supplies and his clumsy daguerreotype equipment. There he met with Frémont and a few key members of the exploring party. They included F. W. von Egloffstein, the chief topographer (the maker of charts and maps), who, like Carvalho, was a Jew. Oliver Fuller was Carvalho's assistant, and there was another photographer named Bomar, whose presence no doubt came as a shock to Carvalho. But Frémont did not want to take any chances with the photographic record, and Bomar's method, a wax process, was entirely different from Carvalho's. Frémont explained that he would choose between the men before the expedition got started. Together, the five men boarded the steamer, F. X. Audrey, bound for Kansas.

By September 15, the entire Frémont party had arrived at Westport (now Kansas City), ready to head westward. While camped there, Frémont got the news that the Heap expedition was already in Colorado and had crossed the Cochetopa Pass. Frémont quickly dismissed this news as unimportant. What had to be proved was that Cochetopa Pass, at the Continental Divide, could be crossed in the dead of winter.

There was still the matter to be decided of who would be the official photographer—Bomar with his wax process or Carvalho, using the daguerreotype method. Frémont held a contest between the two men with speed being the deciding factor. Bomar's wax process required more time and would have caused delays. Carvalho was declared the winner, and he became the expedition's official photographer.

By September 20, all the men going on the expedition had arrived at Westport. The Frémont party consisted of ten Delaware Indians, two Mexicans, several muleskinners, and the officers —von Egloffstein, Oliver Fuller, Max Strobel, W. H. Palmer and Carvalho. The Delawares, all of whom spoke English, had such names as Washington, Welluchas, Solomon and Moses. All were under the command of a Delaware Chief, Captain Wolff, who referred to himself as the "Big Indian." Each man in the party was issued a rifle and a Colt revolver.

The Delawares loved Frémont, their "Great Captain," because he was a firm but fair leader who would not ask a man to take a chance that he himself would not take. Every single one of the Indians would have laid down their lives for him. Therefore, there was great concern and disappointment when Frémont became ill shortly after the expedition left Westport and he had to return to St. Louis for medical treatment. Before leaving, he turned over the command to W. H. Palmer, and left instructions for the expedition to proceed to the Grand Saline Fork of the Kansas River, in Kansas Territory, close to where Sigmund Shlesinger (see chapter I) would distinguish himself fifteen years later at the Battle of Beecher Island.

It was not until late October that Frémont would arrive at the meeting point, fully recovered, to resume his leadership role. Finally ready to proceed, the expedition headed out toward Bent's Fort and the snow-covered peaks of the Rocky Mountains.

The delay caused by Frémont's illness turned out not to be a serious setback. Nothing was lost. A fearsome winter still lay ahead, no matter what. It would take six months for the expedition to reach San Francisco, its destination. To get there, the Frémont party would journey through Kansas, and cut across the lower part of Colorado to Bent's Fort. From there it would cross the Rockies at Cochetopa Pass and march south to the San Juan Mountains in southwest Colorado. Then, after entering Utah, it would cross the dangerous canyonlands into the Mormon settlement at Parowan. The route out of Utah would take the party due west across Nevada to the southern edge of the Sierra Nevada Mountains, and then north to San Francisco.

****

During the journey, Carvalho would have some memorable experiences among the Indians, some pleasant, some harrowing. Certainly, very few Jews had ever marched over the perilous route that Carvalho had crossed, and none, to be sure, had carried cameras.

Shortly after Frémont returned to his men in Kansas Territory, the winter of 1853 began to close in. Carvalho would soon have his first encounter with unfriendly Indians. One especially cold night, Frémont personally inspected the guard, choosing a time when he would be least expected. Finding the guard post unmanned, Frémont asked the officer on duty if he had relieved the guard for any reason. The officer hadn't, but he explained that the cold weather probably accounted for the guard's absence at the exact time Frémont arrived. Surely, it was a coincidence. Probably the guard had gone for a moment to warm his hands at the campfire. Frémont was very angry. He fiercely scolded the officer on

Portrait of Walkara, the Ute chief, painted by the artist,
Solomon Carvalho.
*From the collection of the Gilcrease Museum
Tulsa, Oklahoma*

duty and sentenced the guard to walk the next day instead of riding his mule.

Despite his great admiration for Frémont, Carvalho thought the punishment too harsh. After all, the poor guard had only gone to the campfire to warm his hands. Carvalho found out, however, that the guard's disobedience had had serious results. A party of Cheyenne had evidently been watching the Frémont camp in the night and had stolen five mules in the brief time the guard had left his post. The Delawares later tracked down the Cheyenne and recovered the stolen mules. From then on, Carvalho never questioned an order given by Frémont. The incident had reassured Carvalho that Frémont's watchfulness and experience would help him trek less fearfully through country in which hostile Comanche and Pawnee were always around.

While traveling through Kansas, Carvalho had the chance to make friends with Captain Wolff, the Delaware chief. The chief had fallen ill, and when he noticed some unusual activity taking place in the camp, Carvalho was told by one of the Delawares that a "great medicine man" was performing the Indian ceremony of "incantation" (a ceremonial kind of singing) in an effort to cure the chief. The rite was performed by making an almost-airtight hut of tree branches with just enough room for one man to sit upright inside. The chief, totally naked, sat in the hut, smoking a pipe filled with a mixture of tobacco and "kinnickinick" (dried sumac leaves), puffing frenziedly so that huge drafts of smoke filled his lungs as well as the enclosure. Standing outside the hut, the medicine man recited powerful words while the smoke filled the hut so completely that the poor chief, on the verge of suffocating, had to be carried back to his own tent, gasping for air.

Because he was worried about Captain Wolff, Carvalho entered his tent and found him in a state of great agitation. He believed that his condition was caused by the treatment provided by the medicine man. The chief complained of headache and back pain. He was certain that he was going to die. Carvalho asked that he be given a chance to make the chief well, and, because he had nothing to lose, the chief gladly agreed. Carvalho carried with him an unusual assortment of supplies, including medicines, which were of utmost importance at that moment. He opened his wooden supply box and quickly gave ten grains of calomel to the chief. Four hours later, he returned and gave the Indian a half ounce of Epsom salts. The chief began to recover almost immediately! Carvalho had correctly guessed that the chief was suffering from indigestion.

As soon as he saw the chief responding to his treatment, Carvalho once more reached into the supply box and gave him some arrowroot. He wrote in his diary, "If I had not treated him, he probably would have died." Carvalho had triumphed over the medicine man!

Thanks to the Delaware Indians, Carvalho was gradually able to adjust to camp life. For one thing, he learned how to build a fire with "buffalo chips"—dried dung that burns hot and slowly when it is lighted and retains heat longer than wood. Carvalho wrote, "A peculiar smell exhales from it while burning, and it is not at all unpleasant." The Delawares also taught Carvalho the secret of cooking buffalo meat, of preparing kinnickinick (a good substitute smoke in the absence of tobacco), and of how to excel in playing various Indian games.

The Delawares were great hunters, and during the time they were waiting for Frémont's return from Westport, they had taught Carvalho, who was by then an expert rifle shot, how to hunt buffalo. Early one morning, Carvalho had joined a party of Delawares on a buffalo hunt. After searching patiently for over three hours in the cold autumn morning, Carvalho and the Indians came upon a large herd of the animals, steers, cows and calves alike, and the entire party galloped after them. Because he liked cow meat rather than steer meat (the flesh was more tender), he chased after what he believed to be a cow. After a two mile chase, he fired his rifle, wounding the animal in the leg. Closing in for the kill, he took out his Colt revolver and fired again, only to discover that he had killed an old bull instead. After Carvalho told the story around the campfire that evening, Captain Wolff laughed. He informed Carvalho that he had not killed a buffalo at all, neither bull nor cow. To the Indians, when something is not done according to Indian ritual, then it isn't done at all. The Delaware chief explained: "When Captain Wolff kill buffalo, he cut out tongue. Indian shoot buffalo, bring home tongue. Carvalho no bring buffalo tongue, he no kill buffalo."

As the expedition moved deeper into Kansas Territory, the weather turned cold and unpleasant. For Carvalho to make daguerreotypes in the open air, with temperatures dipping down to thirty below zero, was a far more complicated task than making them in the warm climate of his home state, South Carolina, or the Barbados in the Caribbean, where Carvalho had gained his experience and skill. Despite the fact that the daguerreotype was faster than Bomar's wax process, the heavy weight of the daguerreotype equipment and the slow process in setting it up caused delays in the expedition while Carvalho photographed.

As difficult as the artist's photographic duties were, they did not excuse him from other duties. Carvalho explained in his diary:

The duties of camp life are becoming more onerous as the weather gets colder. It's expected that each man in camp will bring in a certain quantity of firewood! My turn came today, and I'm afraid I shall make a poor hand in using the ax; first, I have not the physical strength, and secondly, I do not know how...I certainly, being a Republican, do not expect to warm myself at the expense of another; therefore, arduous as it is, I must, to carry out the principle of equality, do as the rest do, although it is not a very congenial occupation.

The Frémont expedition followed the Arkansas River, and while on this course, in west-central Kansas, it arrived at a Cheyenne village populated by approximately a thousand men, women, and children, according to Carvalho's estimate. He made daguerreotype pictures of the teepees, and in spite of having a hard time getting the Indians to sit still, he managed to get photographs of an Indian princess, an elderly woman, and several chiefs. He later showed them the daguerreotypes, and from then, he wrote in his diary, "I was a supernatural being."

The Indians were shortly to become convinced beyond doubt that Carvalho was no mere mortal. The Indian princess was a beauty, and for the picture-taking session she had dressed in her finest clothing. She had put on colorful robes, embroidered with elk's teeth, porcupine quills, and beads. On her arms were bracelets of brass, obtained from traders and trappers who had passed through the village. Silver jewelry was rare, and few Indian women, even the daughter of a chief, could claim such a prize. Noting her brass bracelets, Carvalho asked the princess if he might borrow one. Reluctantly she handed it over. He carefully wiped the bracelet clean. Then he took his quicksilver out of the supply box and applied a small amount to the bracelet. The bracelet was instantly changed from brass into what looked like glistening silver. Not believing her eyes and overjoyed at the change in her bracelet, the princess danced with pleasure as she admired the glistening ornament on her arm. other Indian women excitedly gathered around Carvalho, holding their brass bracelets out to the artist, and soon he became the great magician, the man who could miraculously change brass to silver. The astonished Indians pleaded with Carvalho to stay on and live among them forever.

While he was with the Cheyennes, Carvalho witnessed an impressive sight: the return of the Cheyenne warriors from a successful battle with the Pawnees, their deadliest enemies. As part of the celebration, the Cheyenne performed a scalp dance, in which more than a dozen Pawnee scalps, dangling from poles, were the center of the victory celebration. The men and women of the village wore wolf, bear, and buffalo robes, and deer antlers and buffalo horns for head ornaments.

They danced and chanted around a huge fire, their faces streaked with red and black paint. Carvalho watched the strange and scary ceremony without showing any feeling. He concluded only that the Indians simply had no instinct for music because they all sang in monotone.

About seventy miles east of the Rockies, close to where Lamar, Colorado, is now located, was the site of Bent's Fort. At that time, it was new and was also an important Santa Fe Trail outpost for traders, Indians, and trappers. Farther to the west, the original fort had been destroyed by its owner, William Bent, after a dispute with the government. The expedition stayed for a short time at the new fort while Frémont stocked up with supplies—fresh mules for each man, dried buffalo meat, overshoes, sugar, coffee, and buffalo robes. The cold was already bitter and would get worse. Frémont and his men would need all the food and cold weather gear William Bent could provide.

Their supplies in hand, the expedition now proceeded across the Huerfano River toward the base of the Rockies, where they could see the glistening white summit of Pike's Peak off in the distant northwest. While there, Carvalho and Frémont left the party to search for impressive scenes to photograph. Among the pictures were Huerfano Butte, and off in the distance, San Luis Valley and the San Juan Mountains. Some of the views were so spectacular that they could be improved upon only by scaling snow-covered peaks. Frémont wanted all the views, but he did not want to climb farther. Carvalho himself, however, insisted on climbing higher because he was so stunned by the breathtaking view of the Rockies.

> Standing as it were in the vestibule of God's holy temple, I forgot I was of this mundane sphere; the divine part of man elevated itself undisturbed by the influences of the world. I looked from nature up to nature's God, more chastened and purified than I ever felt before.

The expedition inched its way up the Sangre de Cristo Mountains, and then into the San Luis Valley, finally Cochetopa Pass on December 14, 1853. Frémont, Egloffstein, Fuller and Strobel took the necessary sightings and made sketches for their maps.

Carvalho took numerous daguerreotypes. Having reached the Continental Divide, the expedition would have to make its descent. Icy winds and heavy snow would make the long climb down to Colorado's western slope very dangerous. To add to its problems, the expedition's food supply was beginning to run out. On New Year's day, 1854, Carvalho, who had not as yet exhausted his bag of tricks, pulled out a surprise.

Jewish Heroes of the Wild West

He had brought with him two boxes of preserved eggs and milk in sealed tin cans. No one knew he had these rare items. In honor of New Year's day, he combined sugar, milk, and eggs with six gallons of boiling water, and "made as fine a blanc mange (a kind of vanilla pudding) as ever was manged on Mount Blanc (in Europe)...six gallons of nourishing food, sweetened and flavored," enough to serve each man on the expedition.

****

The Frémont party was again underway. It moved slowly across the western slope of Colorado and crossed the Grand River at the Colorado-Utah frontier. The men were now a ragged group. Frémont, the even-tempered leader, did his best to encourage the men, but they were tired and miserably cold. More and more they were becoming concerned with their own survival. In a few days, they would reach the red canyonlands of eastern Utah and cross the Green River, but by then they would have shot all twenty-seven of their horses for food and would journey the rest of the way on foot, in bitter cold, in their worn-out boots.

With the worst still to come, Carvalho, the snow above his knees, made his way up the mountain slope to round up the stray horses. He reached under his buffalo robes and pulled out a miniature (small picture) of his wife and children.

Gazing sadly at the picture and bitterly regretting his decision to accompany Frémont on the expedition, he thought of his mother and her words. "Dear Soul, how her heart would have ached for him…"

Cold, tired, and hungry, he made his way back to camp. He warmed his hands before the fire and lay down under his buffalo robes, thinking of "warm rooms," "feather beds," and the "silken canopy" of his wedding chamber.

The scientific duties of Egloffstein, Fuller and Carvalho made it necessary for them to bring up the rear of the party. By now, the group was approaching the Green River. Fuller could not go on any longer. He had been on foot more than any other member of the party, his horse having been shot for food after the animal had collapsed. His boots were so worn out that the flesh of his feet was exposed. Because of his condition, Carvalho and Egloffstein had no choice but to leave their comrade behind while they sought help. They too were traveling on foot, burdened with their equipment. When Frémont heard of Fuller's problem, he sent two Delawares to rescue him, but by the time Fuller was returned to camp, it was too late. His frostbitten legs were black, and even if he had lived, they would have had to be amputated. Fuller had been the strongest man in the camp when they left Westport and seemed to be much bet-

ter prepared for hardships than any other man. Carvalho thought it was very ironic that he himself, the weakest of them all, was alive to write about Fuller's sufferings and death.

On February 8, 1854, the expedition finally reached Parowan, Utah, a small Mormon settlement in the Little Salt Lake Valley. Salt Lake City was three hundred miles to the north, San Bernardino, California, five hundred miles southwest. Parowan's population when Frémont's ragged party staggered into the village was one hundred Mormon families.

The expedition had suffered through heavy snow drifts, freezing cold, and intense hunger. They were tired and skinny. Carvalho was ill, with symptoms of diarrhea and scurvy (a disease caused by lack of vitamin C). His clothes were torn, his hair long and tangled, and he had become as thin as a skeleton. The people of Parowan mistook him for an Indian. The most difficult part of the journey was over, but neither Carvalho nor Egloffstein were in any condition to continue with Frémont, and they had to leave the expedition.

Frémont and his men stayed on in Parowan for two weeks. During that time, the men were fed and clothed by the Mormons, and Carvalho's health improved. It was while they were there that Frémont learned that the Gunnison expedition had failed, and that John Gunnison himself had been killed by Indians.

The day Frémont left Parowan, Carvalho and Egloffstein, both still not fully recovered, set out for Salt Lake City. They rode in a wagon with a group of Mormons on their way to "conference" (a religious meeting). Carvalho remained in Salt Lake City for ten weeks where he gradually regained his health. He got on very well with the Mormons, and although he did not believe in their practice of polygamy (men having more than one wife), he saw that the Mormons had many admirable qualities. The city of Salt Lake itself told the story. It had a population of fifteen thousand. During his stay, Carvalho was pleasantly surprised that he never heard any obscene language, never saw anybody drunk, saw no dance halls or gambling dens.

While in Salt Lake, Egloffstein, the topographical engineer, accepted a job with Lieutenant Beckwith of the Gunnison expedition, replacing an engineer who had been killed by the Indians.

The territory of Utah, which included Nevada and western Colorado, was organized in 1850, and Brigham Young was appointed governor. Young was successful in bringing peace to various warring tribes, and Carvalho thought he had made headway in soothing the hostile feelings of Indians towards white immigrants. However, Young was not successful in converting the Indians to the Mormon religion, and all the kindness he extended to Carvalho was not performed in an attempt to convert him, either. The Mormons believe Jews are God's chosen people, and they identify their members as descendants of Abraham, Isaac, and Jacob, so that conversion becomes unnecessary.

Young, who had nineteen wives and countless children, took Carvalho under his wing and invited the artist to live in his home. During Carvalho's stay, Young invited him to attend a grand ball. Despite the fact that his own clothes were in shreds and, even if they were in good condition, would have been inappropriate for such an occasion, he somehow managed to appear as fashionably dressed as any man there. The resourceful artist had somehow obtained striped "cassimere" (cashmere) trousers, a black frock coat, and a white vest.

The day of the ball, Carvalho had dinner at the home of Ezra Taft Benson, where Benson's wives were busily preparing food—roasting wild geese, baking, and "garnishing fat hams" for the ball.

Young graciously gave Carvalho a general introduction at the ball, and invited the artist to dance with one of his wives. "A larger collection of fairer and more beautiful women I never saw in one room," Carvalho wrote. But, he added, "the utmost order and strictest decorum prevailed." Polkas and waltzes and other "partner dances" were not permitted, but quadrilles and cotillions as well as other forms of country dances, like square dances, were allowed.

While in Salt Lake City, Carvalho painted several portraits—two of Brigham Young, and several of officials of the Mormon Church.

On May 6, 1854, Carvalho left Salt Lake, bound for San Bernardino and Los Angeles. Young wanted Carvalho to have a safe escort, so the artist left with a party of twenty-three Mormon missionaries. Their route would take them on a southwest course through various Mormon settlements in Utah. Along the way there would be a brief meeting with Young in Provost City (Provo). The governor had promised to wait for Carvalho there before having a parley with Walkara, the great Ute Indian chief. Relations had been strained between the Mormons and the Indians, resulting in bloody clashes with deaths on both sides. Captain John Gunnison was killed in revenge for the wanton slaying of an Indian by white immigrants on their way to California. The Utahs (Utes), the Paiutes, and the Pavants (Indians of that area) were committed to revenge against all white men, including the Mormons. But Major Biddell, the Indian agent, had been able to persuade the Indians to suspend their war on the white man until Brigham Young, the great white leader, could meet Walkara, the great Ute Chief.

Carvalho wrote of eventually catching up with Young at a Mormon settlement nineteen miles south of Provost City, and of being greeted warmly by the Mormon leader. In Young's party were Ezra Taft Benson, along with several apostles and advisers, "fifty men on mounts and one hundred wagons and teams filled with gentlemen with their wives and families." Completing the party was the Jew, Solomon Carvalho. The tribal chiefs, together with the Young party, were to meet at Walkara's camp outside the village of Nephi.

Young brought with him an assortment of valuable gifts for the Indians—sixteen head of cattle, blankets, clothing, trinkets, even arms and ammunition. Carvalho questioned Young about the wisdom of furnishing arms to the Indians, but Young replied that the purpose was to give the Indians the means of shooting their own game. Besides, Young, added, the Indians were already well-armed and quite expert in the use of rifles.

Young sent word of his arrival to Walkara, hinting that Walkara might meet him at the Young encampment outside of Provost City. Walkara would have none of that. His attitude was that since he had been the injured party in all the fighting, he did not care very much what the outcome of their meeting might be. He promptly sent back word that, if the governor wished to see him, he would have to come to Walkara.

When the Young party finally arrived, they were greeted by such famous chiefs as Ammon, Squash-Head, Grosepine, Petetnit, and Kanosh. They were then invited into Walkara's tent, Carvalho going in with them.

Walkara, wrapped in a blanket and sitting on his buffalo robes, waved to Young and motioned him to sit at his side.

Jewish Heroes of the Wild West

After introductions were made, the chiefs immediately began to vent their anger, describing in detail all their complaints against the Mormons and other white men, recounting tales of Indian women having been murdered and of sons killed in battle. Young made his plea for peace. Walkara remained silent, but finally announced that he would consult with the Great Spirit and render a decision on the following day.

When the peace parley resumed the next day, Walkara was very tired. He had spent the night carefully examining all sides of the issue. Should the Indians declare war on the Mormons and all other white men, or should there be peace? He said to Young that he had been wrongly accused of killing Captain Gunnison, an accusation which made him "sore at heart." Nevertheless, the Great Spirit had advised: "Make peace. When Mormon first come to live on Walkara's land, Walkara give him welcome. He give Walkara plenty bread and clothes…Walkara no want to fight Mormon. Mormon chief very good man."

With Walkara's decision delivered, the peace pipe was passed around, and the council concluded. Carvalho, in the meantime, had been sketching the various chiefs, and later he persuaded Walkara to sit for a portrait, the same portrait that today hangs at the Gilcrease Museum in Tulsa, Oklahoma.

Jewish Heroes of the Wild West

When they left Walkara's camp, Carvalho and the Young party set out for Fillmore City, thirty-five miles to the south. There Carvalho, accompanied by two interpreters, headed straight for the Pavant Indian camp to see Kanosh, their chief, because Carvalho wanted to paint his portrait. He wrote of their meeting:

> I found him well-armed with a rifle and pistols and mounted on a noble horse. He has a Roman nose with fine intelligent cast of countenance, and his thick black hair is brushed off his forehead, contrary to the usual custom of the table. He immediately consented to my request that he would sit for his portrait, and on the spot, after an hour's labor, I produced a strong likeness of him which he was very curious to see. I opened my portfolio and displayed portraits of a number of chiefs, among which he selected Walkara. He took hold of it and wanted to retain it. It was, he said, "weino"—a contraction of the Spanish "bueno"—very good.

The Pavant chief then told Carvalho the details surrounding the massacre of Captain Gunnison. It was actually his own tribe, the Pavants, who had done it, although Kanosh himself was not involved. Gunnison's death, however, was justified, the chief pointed out, because it was an act of revenge for the death of an old Pavant chief by one of Gunnison's party.

Carvalho continued his journey south, finally reaching Parowan, the small Mormon settlement where he first arrived, cold and emaciated, after his journey over the mountains with Frémont. The same people who cared for him during his illness a few months earlier were on hand to greet him. They were, of course, a bit startled to see a much more robust and healthy Carvalho, and at first they had not recognized him.

The day after he arrived, Carvalho, while taking a stroll through the village, his sketchbook in his hand, noticed a man pacing nervously back and forth, in front of a small shack. Carvalho approached him and asked what was wrong. The man told him his only daughter, six years old, had died suddenly during the night, and asked Carvalho to step inside the shack.

Carvalho spotted the child's dead body lying on a straw mattress, and he was struck by her beauty. "She was one of the most angelic children I ever saw," he wrote,"…beautiful curls clustered around a brow of snowy whiteness. It was easy to perceive that it was a child lately from England from its peculiar conformation." The child's mother was reclining on a bed, sobbing into her pillow.

Carvalho immediately began sketching the child. His hand was drawn to his sketch pad as if by some outside force, so overcome was he by the child's beauty. In a short time he had produced an excellent likeness of the little girl. The mother, who had not seen Carvalho come into the room, now took notice of him. He explained that he was part of the Brigham Young party, having arrived the evening before. With that, he handed the mother his sketch of her daughter. "It is impossible to describe the delight and joy expressed at its possession," Carvalho wrote. "She said I was an angel sent from heaven to comfort her. She had no likeness of her child."

The next day, while Carvalho was preparing for his journey to San Bernardino, he found a basket filled with eggs, butter, and several loaves of bread in his wagon. A note was in the basket. It read: "From a grateful heart."

Carvalho eventually reached Los Angeles where, during his short visit, he was instrumental in forming the Los Angeles Hebrew Benevolent Society. At its first meeting, the society passed a resolution of thanks in Carvalho's honor:

> Los Angeles, California—At a meeting of the Israelites of the city of Los Angeles, held on this 2nd of July, 1854, for the purpose of forming a charitable society by the name of "Hebrew Benevolent Society" and for the purpose of obtaining a piece of land for a Jewish graveyard, the following officers were elected: S. K. Labatt, President; Charles Shachro, Vice President; Hyam Goldberg and S. Lazard, Trustees; and Jacob Elias, Secretary.

It was resolved unanimously that the thanks of this meeting be tendered to Mr. S. N. Carvalho for his valuable services in organizing the Society, and that he be elected an honorary member; also, that these proceedings be published in The Occident (a Jewish publication of the time).

After leaving Parowan on February 21, 1854, Colonel Frémont and his party (Carvalho and Egloffstein, its two Jewish members, absent), followed the wagon route to Cedar City, Utah, then moved toward the Escalante Desert, entering Nevada near the village of Pioche. The expedition reached the Sierra Nevada range at what is now Bishop, California, eventually arriving at the San Joachin Valley and then San Francisco.

Frémont hailed his expedition as a success. His trailblazing journey would serve well as a year 'round railroad route. A major advantage of the route was that along the way there were big stands of timber in addition to rich deposits of coal and iron. The human cost of the expedition, however, had been a heavy one. Provisions were scanty and the men went hungry for days at a time. Pack animals went lame and were eventually eaten. The scientist, Fuller, had died on the trail.

Solomon Nunes Carvalho had come from an old Sephardic Jewish family whose origins were Spanish and Portuguese. The family had lived in England for several generations.

Carvalho's father, David Nunes Carvalho, also an artist as well as a man of literary taste, was born in London in 1784. In 1814, he married Sarah D'Azevedo of Charleston, South Carolina, and a year later, on April 27, 1815, the first child, Solomon was born. David and Sarah had four more children during the next twenty years—Emmanuel, Isaac, Sarah, and Julia. Isaac, the last born, did not survive infancy.

Carvalho was reared in Charleston, at that time a prosperous port and center of trade and culture. He was educated at Charleston College and at local religious schools. Well-grounded in the classics, he knew Latin, Greek, and Hebrew. David and Sarah, his parents, placed great value on secular and Jewish culture, and Carvalho, throughout his life, pursued these interests with great enthusiasm. Between 1828 and 1860, he moved around a great deal, living for various periods in Philadelphia, Baltimore, Charleston, Barbados (in the Caribbean), Los Angeles, and New York. After his father's death in 1860, he moved his family permanently to New York. Carvalho was then forty-five. In New York he would achieve the financial success he had never had as an artist by opening a steam and hot water heating business, using products that he himself had invented.

David and Sarah Carvalho had moved from Charleston to Baltimore in 1828, when Solomon was thirteen. Seven years later, the family moved once again, this time to Philadelphia. Solomon, now approaching twenty, was sent to Barbados to live with and work for an uncle in the importing business. In 1838, while still living in Barbados, he sold his first painting, an interior of the Charleston synagogue which he had painted from memory. It would be the first of well over sixty of his works—portraits and landscapes, photographs and sketches—that exist today in various public and private collections. His portrait of Abraham Lincoln, commissioned by the president and among his best known, is at the American Jewish Historical Society. A portrait of Judah Touro hangs at the Touro Infirmary in New Orleans; his celebrated portrait of Walkara, the chief's hair brushed down on his forehead, has a startling effect on visitors to the Gilcrease Museum.

Other portraits include those of Brigham Young; Judah P. Benjamin, the Confederate patriot; Dr. David Camden DeLeon, first surgeon general of the Confederate army; Don Pio Pico, Spanish governor of California; Paul Morphy, the American chess grandmaster, friend and occasional chess opponent of Carvalho; and Isaac Leeser, the Sephardic rabbi, editor of THE OCCIDENT and spiritual force behind the founding of Dropsie College, in Philadelphia.

Several of Carvalho's paintings were rendered from sketches on his expedition with Frémont. These include "View in the

Cochetopa Pass, Rocky Mountains, Discovered by Colonel Freemont;" "Entrance to the Valley of St. Clare, Between Utah and California;" and "Sunset on the Los Angeles River." Most of Carvalho's photography and sketches of the expedition were lost and have never been located, although it is said that some plates are still in unopened crates at the National Archives, mixed with those of Matthew Brady, the Civil War photographer.

Carvalho's painting, "Child with Rabbits," later was used as an embellishment on widely-circulated bank notes in the United States and Canada in the 1850's and 1860's.

Carvalho not only invented a heating process but also a process to protect daguerreotype plates. Isaac Leeser wrote in THE OCCIDENT:

> Mr. S. N. Carvalho has invented a method of varnishing daguerreotypes which will protect them against abrasion and dispense with the necessity of covering them with glass. It is not often that persons of our persuasion turn their attention to inventions and mechanical contrivances; wherefore we seize the first leisure we have to record them in our magazine.

****

Carvalho, the writer, was a contributor to the THE OCCIDENT. In addition, he wrote long essays on religious subjects, including one called "The Mosaic Cosmogony," which refers to the picture of the universe described in the first five books of the Bible. In addition to his book, INCIDENTS OF TRAVEL, he was the author of a history of the Isle of Martinique (the French Caribbean), which appeared in HARPER'S MONTHLY.

Owing to his association with Frémont, Carvalho's INCIDENTS OF TRAVEL became an instant success when it first appeared in 1856. When the publisher offered him a choice of a flat payment of three hundred dollars or royalties of five cents per copy, Carvalho accepted the flat payment because he needed money at that time. His decision was unfortunate because the book proved to be such a great success.

In 1845, nine years before he left for the West, Carvalho had married Sarah Marion Solis, fourth daughter of Jacob Fonseca D'Silva Solis, whose ancestry dated back to twelfth century Spain.

Their wedding notice in THE OCCIDENT read:

> On Wednesday, the 15th of October, at the residence of Mr. S. Solis, Mr. Solomon N. Carvalho of Bridgetown, Barbados, and son of Mr. D. N. Carvalho of Philadelphia, to Miss Sarah M. Solis of the city, daughter of the late Jacob S. Solis.

Sarah's father was dead, so Solomon had to turn to her brother to seek her hand in marriage. Carvalho's elegant writing style was never clearer than in his letter to Solomon Solis:

> For your esteemed sister, Sarah, I have conceived other than mere commonplace feelings. Her amiability, sweetness of temper, together with a congeniality of disposition and I dare hope a reciprocity of sentiment, have awakened in my bosom feelings of a deep and ardent affection and as her guardian and Elder Brother, I deem it a duty I owe you, to acquaint you with my pretensions, and to obtain your sanction that I may make her Honorable proposals of Marriage, the consummation of which would render me most happy.

After his marriage, Carvalho began seriously to devote himself to art and photography. He gained some acclaim during the next several years but not much wealth. His reputation as an artist and daguerreotypist reached Frémont, and eight years after his marriage, he would say good-bye to Sarah and their three young children, David, Jacob, and Charity and, at the age of thirty-eight, begin his memorable journey over the Rockies

In 1855, the newly-formed Republican party asked Frémont, after his fifth expedition, to be a candidate for president. He was thought to be the ideal choice. The Republicans took a strong position against slavery just as Frémont had, and because of his successful explorations, Frémont had become a romantic hero to most Americans. He was officially nominated on June 19, 1856, at the Republican convention in Philadelphia. His running mate, Senator William L. Dayton of New Jersey, edged out Abraham Lincoln for second place on the ticket. The other presidential candidates were James Buchanan for the Democrats and Millard Fillmore for the Whigs.

Frémont was a quiet and thoughtful man, more at home around a campfire than on the campaign trail. He was made popular and glorified by such well-known journalists of the day as Horace Greeley and John Greenleaf Whittier, also known as one of the "bearded New Englanders," among the best-loved American poets of the late nineteenth century. Frémont, who wanted to discuss serious matters of the day, could not develop the kind of style most politicians employ to win votes and impress their constituents—that is, he could not become a different kind of man from the one he was.

Meanwhile, Carvalho was gaining a benefit from Frémont's campaign. In New York, at the time his book INCIDENTS OF TRAVEL was published, Carvalho campaigned vigorously for Frémont. He addressed Frémont's supporters in large street gatherings and basked in Frémont's glory. "Three cheers for Carvalho, the Frémont expedition artist," the crowds would yell. "Hip, Hip,

Hooray!" Flushed by the success of his book, Carvalho began to enjoy life in New York, dining in elegant restaurants and smoking "a dozen four-cent cigars daily," having a great time with his newfound fame. If Frémont became president, Carvalho expected to be appointed Collector of the Port of Baltimore.

Regrettably, it was not to be. Frémont's opponents slammed him without pity—for his illegitimate birth, for his Catholic upbringing (even though he himself was an Episcopalian), and for his failed fourth expedition. He lost the election to Buchanan, who carried nineteen states. Frémont carried eleven, Fillmore eight. Even though he did not win, Frémont had made a respectable showing.

From the time of his defeat until the outbreak of the Civil War, Frémont and his wife Jessie lived a quiet and fashionable life in San Francisco. When the war broke out, he was commissioned a major general in the Union Army, commanding the Department of the West, with headquarters in St. Louis. Frémont, first and always a dreamer and trailblazer, had the misfortune to confront Stonewall Jackson in battle, and even though their battle was an impossibly difficult one, his defeat resulted in disgrace. Lincoln, now president, placed Frémont's troops under the command of General John Pope.

Because of Frémont's popularity, his dismissal by Lincoln was not politically wise, and the president assigned him to another post. In March, 1862, he was named commander of the Mountain Department. Unfortunately, this assignment was also ill-fated, and again Frémont lost his appointment.

After the war, because of a series of poor business ventures, Frémont's financial position grew desperate. He lived off the writings of his wife, Jessie, and a small salary as territorial governor of Arizona. After he died penniless in 1890, John Charles Frémont nevertheless continued to be a symbol of freedom and adventure to the American people. Until the very last, Frémont, the trailblazer of the West, kept on dreaming of further expeditions.

Carvalho, who made his home in New York after 1861, was in New Orleans at the outbreak of the Civil War. The reason for his trip was to introduce his new steam-heating process to the South, and also to try to sell prayer books for Isaac Leeser while there, as well as soliciting subscriptions in the Jewish community for Leeser's periodical, THE OCCIDENT. It was during this trip that he painted the portrait of Judah Touro.

His process for heating with hot water and steam eventually became quite successful. It was promoted as "An Entirely

New Steam Super-Heating System By Hot Water Circulating Under Pressure." The invention won Carvalho the Medal of Excellence by the American Institute of New York. He began calling himself "Professor," and became president of the Carvalho Heating Company in New York in 1867. He continued to paint until 1870 when failing eyesight ended his career as an artist.

In 1897, at the age of eighty-two, Solomon Nunes Carvalho, official artist and photographer for Frémont's fifth expedition, died peacefully in New York. His paintings and photographs, which are valued treasures today in libraries, museums, and private collections, tell only a part of this Jewish Leonardo (Leonardo da Vinci, the painter and sculptor of the Italian Renaissance). To those who cherish the exploits of the trailblazing heroes of the West, Carvalho, the man who painted Indians, was also one of the first Jews to cross the Rockies, a Jewish medicine man who saved the life of a chief, a man who hunted buffalo with the Indians, who magically transformed brass bracelets into silver, and who sat with Brigham Young and Chief Walkara at the truce powwow between the Mormons and the Utes.

****

He and his wife Sarah, who died three years before him, are buried in Shearith Israel Synagogue cemetery in New York— a long, long way from Cochetopa Pass.

UNCLE JULIUS'S LAST WALK

Julius Meyer with Chief Standing Bear
American Jewish Archives

UNCLE JULIUS'S LAST WALK

On a spring morning in 1909, a smartly-dressed sixty-year-old bachelor, the general agent in Omaha, Nebraska, for the Provident Life Assurance Society (a well-known insurance company), left his comfortable apartment over Adler's store at Twelfth and Farnam Streets. He strolled down Farnam until he reached his brother Moritz's cigar store. He stopped and chatted with his brother, bought a cigar, lighted it, and said, contentedly, "Well, I think I will walk up the street a while and get some fresh air."

He was in good spirits because he was feeling better after a case of ptomaine poisoning. Living in Omaha for more than forty years, he had seen the city grow from a few thousand people to over 70,000. The city had developed into an important railroad center after the completion of the Union Pacific Railroad, which was followed by the Rock Island, the Burlington, and the Northwestern. Because of the city's rise as a major railroad center, he had also seen the growth of the meat-packing industry.

He walked out of his brother's store with the self-assurance of someone who had become successful. Rising from a poor immigrant German Jew to a beloved, wealthy man in an important developing American city, he took notice of the changes in his lifetime. The frame shacks which used to occupy Farnam Street had been replaced by tall buildings with several storeys. The city was prosperous, and he himself had contributed to its prosperity.

After walking a few steps up Farnam, he paused, turned, and waved to his brother. It was 10:30 in the morning on May 10, 1909, and he was about to take the last walk of his life.

Only an hour and a half later, just before noon, his body was found lying beside a bench in Hanscom Park, two miles from his brother's store. Two bullets had pierced his body, and he clutched a revolver in his left hand. His death was finally ruled a suicide; the reason given was that he had been depressed because of ill health.

Julius Meyer, the man who died in Hanscom Park, was outgoing and well-liked. He was one of Omaha's most spirited citizens. It was he who had organized the Standard Club, the first social club of any importance in Omaha. He had been one of the founders of Temple Beth Israel, and he was an active member of the Hebrew Benevolent Society. A music lover and an accomplished musician, he played the fute and the violin;

he also organized a 117-piece orchestra known as the Omaha Musicians Union, which he himself had sometimes conducted. As the best-known patron of the arts in his home town of Omaha, he frequently entertained some of Europe's most famous singers and musicians.

To his nieces and nephews, as well as many of the children of Omaha, he was simply known as Uncle Julius. But some forty years earlier, he had been known as "Box-Ka-Re-Sha-Hash-Ta-Ka," a name given to him by the Pawnees who had adopted him into their tribe. The Indian name meant: "curly-headed white chief who speaks with one tongue."

Julius Meyer was a man with many talents. At the beginning, he was an Indian trader, operating the "Indian Wigwam," a trading post on Farnam Street. He ran his business there from the late 1860's until the last years of the nineteenth century. As a lad of sixteen, during the early days of his trading, Meyer served General George Crook, who was at that time the commander of the Department of the Platte. Julius Meyer acted as an interpreter, for in only a short time he had learned to speak seven Indian dialects—Ponca, Brule, Sioux, Omaha, Winnebago, Pawnee, and Oglala Sioux. Standing Bear, Red Cloud, Sitting Bull, and other chiefs were among his friends.

In addition, he was very skillful in presenting Indians to white society. We can imagine how fascinating Indians were to both Americans and Europeans, who wanted to learn about their clothing, customs and artifacts. Julius was able to make good use of that fascination.

The circumstances surrounding his death remind one of an Agatha Christie story—mysterious, shadowy, nerve-racking. To some people questions continue to arise to this very day. It is ironic that in his death Uncle Julius receives attention, just as he thrived on attention during his lifetime.

Uncle Julius Meyer's story is typical of the early years of Jewish migration to the West. The first of those immigrants came to the Nebraska Territory in the early 1860's, attracted by the population growth which followed the completion of the Union Pacific railroad. Most of these immigrants had come from Austria and Hungary, as well as Germany. They settled in Omaha. While many of them remained there, others followed the railroad route west, eventually settling in Grand Island, Frémont, Columbus, and North Platte.

In 1860, Omaha's population was 1,880, but in ten years it had grown to 16,000. Between 1863 and 1865, as the population began expanding, three immigrant brothers from Blomberg in Germany arrived in Omaha—Max, Moritz, and Adolph Meyer, who were the elder brothers of Julius. In 1866, Omaha was granted its city charter and Nebraska achieved statehood.

Led by Max, the eldest of the Meyer brothers, they wasted no time going into business. Each day new faces appeared on Farnam Street, for the Meyers had many things to sell and there was no shortage of buyers. Max's first business venture, which he operated with his brother Moritz, was called Max Meyer and Bro. Co., founded in 1866 as a cigar store, on Farnam near Eleventh Street. In the meantime, Adolph started a jewelry and music business on Twelfth and Douglas. In 1869, the two businesses merged and moved into a building at the northwest corner of Eleventh and Farnam.

Julius had come to the United States in 1864, when he was only thirteen years old. (In those days it was very common for very young children to leave Europe for America, for necessity made them grow up much more quickly than children in our country today. Many children, even younger than thirteen, were already helping to support families who relied on their meager wages for the most simple things of life).

A little over a year after his arrival Omaha, which was then a small, dusty settlement on the edge of the prairie, Julius began to trade with the Indians. He would trade trinkets from Max's jewelry store and cigars made by his brother Moritz in return for Indian products. It was while he was engaged in these trading activities that Julius learned the languages of the various Indians with whom he dealt.

Julius's "Indian Wigwam" was probably just another branch of Max Meyer and Bro. Co. Julius called himself a dealer in "Indian, Chinese, and Japanese Curiosities," so we conclude that the oriental objects had been obtained through Max's suppliers. These imported articles increased business at the trading post, even though they were different from the Indian image by which the post was known. Julius obtained the Indian wares from his Indian friends, and included beads, moccasins, scalps, peace pipes and furs and skins of animals they had caught and processed for sale. Because more and more people were traveling to Omaha and beyond, the "Indian Wigwam" quickly became an important tourist attraction.

During his trips into Indian country, Julius would travel on foot or horseback. Often he lived with the Indians for weeks, bedding down in their teepees or wigwams. Naturally, the Indians appreciated him because he knew their language so well. Few white men had taken so much trouble to learn it. Another important reason for Julius's success among the

Indians was his honesty in dealing with them. His Indian name, "Box-Ka-Re-Sha-Hash-Ta-Ka" ("Curly-headed white chief who speaks with one tongue"), is evidence of his integrity. (Often we hear the term "speak with forked tongue" which Indians might use to describe someone who said one thing and did something else.)

Julius's relations with the Indians were social as well as commercial. Often he would be invited to Indian dog feasts, where the main course was the boiled carcass of a dog. These feasts were special occasions, and it was an honor for a white man to be invited. However, because he observed the Jewish laws of Kashrut, he could not eat dog meat. Respecting his observance, the Indians served him hard-boiled eggs, for they had learned from their experience with other traders that eggs presented no dietary problems.

At an early age, Julius had the instincts of a showman. It is told that, on one of his trading missions, he took along a show-business friend, a magician known as Herman the Great. He performed for the Indians, and dazzled them with his magic tricks. One trick in particular amazed the Indian audience. Herman extracted gold pieces with great flourish, seemingly out of his empty hat. That night, two Indians crept into the tepee where Julius and Herman slept, intending to scalp the magician in order to get their hands on Herman's magic hat. Fortunately, Julius awakened in time to prevent the assault.

Julius's trading trips were never entirely without danger. On one trip he was confronted by a party of unfriendly Indians who had seized his pack and were ready to scalp him. Pawnee Chief Standing Bear came upon the scene just in the nick of time and helped to save Julius's life. That incident was the beginning of a friendship that would last between the two for the rest of their lives.

Julius Meyer Store, Omaha.
Nebraska State Historical Society

Lena Rehfeld, Julius's niece, later recalled that her uncle carried a scar on his forehead as a reminder of that episode. As for Standing Bear, "Uncle Julius never forgot him for that, and Standing Bear never wanted for anything while he lived that Uncle Julius could provide for him."

Julius did make good use of his friendship for commercial gain. Newspaper advertisements for the "Indian Wigwam" promoted Julius as an Indian trader and interpreter, and always included his Indian name. One of the most dramatic and profitable plans he thought up was to arrange for photographs with his Indian friends. In these photographs, Julius posed with such celebrated chiefs as Standing Bear, also Red Cloud and Sitting Bull, both of whom were Oglala Sioux. Swift Bear and Spotted Tail were Brule Sioux. In one photograph, Julius is dressed up in ornate ceremonial Indian garb. He posed sitting before a campfire, a peace pipe in his hand, surrounded by six Indian warriors, each naked down to the waist.

Julius paid the Indians well for posing. In another famous photograph, Julius, again in Indian dress, stands next to Red Cloud, while seated in front are Sitting Bull, Swift Bear, and Spotted Tail. This picture is said to have cost Julius $800, a tremendous sum in those days, for he had to bring the chiefs to Omaha and give each of them two ponies for posing. This picture, as well as others in which Julius posed with Indians, tells us something strange about the nineteenth century—the Indians liked wearing white men's clothing and the white man occasionally enjoyed donning Indian attire. Julius's youthful face, sporting a black mustache from under an Indian headdress or coonskin cap, left little doubt which figure in the photos was Jewish and which was Indian!

The practice of cross-dressing between Caucasians and Indians was not an invention of Julius, but can be traced back to colonial times when the British presented the Indians with silver medals, decorated collars, and military coats. Later, when Merriwether Lewis and William Clark confronted the Sioux chief, Weucha, in what is now South Dakota, they presented him with a military coat worn by the United States Artillery Corps. In 1839, a St. Louis doctor met a Sioux warrior wearing a red English uniform, and in the same year, William Ferris, a mountain man, ran across a large party of Teton Dakotas on the Platte (River). Several wore long scarlet coats trimmed with gold and silver lace. Coats of this type later became known as "chief's coats." This chief's coat, which is rarely seen today except in museums, was styled like a military frock coat, and was regarded as a status symbol by the Indians. It was fashionable, expensive, and, above all, it was worn by the white military whom the Indians respected.

Jewish Heroes of the Wild West

Julius Meyer with Indian Chiefs. (Standing): Meyer, Red Cloud; (Seated) Sitting Bull, Swift Bear, Spotted Tail, c. 1869
Nebraska State Historical Society

In their photograph with Julius, Red Cloud, Swift Bear, and Spotted Tail wore versions of the chief's coat and for an added touch of elegance, Swift Bear and Spotted Tail hold stove pipe hats in their hands. Strangely enough, it is only Julius and Sitting Bull who wear Indian costumes!

Julius was only one of many white men who dressed up in Indian clothing. The men who did so needed to establish some bond with the Indians or were showmen. Lewis posed for his portrait in genuine Nez Perce clothing, and George Armstrong Custer posed in Indian dress in a photograph taken at Fort Abraham Lincoln. He even went into battle on the Little Big Horn wearing a buckskin coat and fringed buckskin breeches. Lieutenant Stephen Hills, who commanded a company of Chiricahua scouts, wore Apache clothing to gain the confidence of his troops. Both Dan Beard, one of the founders of the Boy Scouts, and Theodore Roosevelt, a United States president, were photographed wearing Indian clothing.

As a showman, Julius was well aware of the commercial value of establishing close ties with the Indians. By posing for photographs in Indian outfits, he wanted to create the impression that he was a genuine frontiersman, a man deeply involved with the Indians and inseparable from them and their culture. This was the same image that other celebrated showmen—Buffalo Bill, Deadeye Dick, Annie Oakley, Deadwood Dick and Buckskin Jack—tried to create by wearing Indian buckskin.

During the late nineteenth century, the white men in the East and in Europe were spellbound by the American Indian. Julius recognized an opportunity when he saw it, and he took a party of Indians for public appearances on one or two occasions. The reports of these trips present a mixed picture;

one source states that Julius took a group of Omahas and Winnebagos to the Paris Exposition of 1883, where they remained for three months. But in an article of the NATIONAL JEWISH MONTHLY, Julius is said to have taken his Indian friends, Standing Bear included, to the Paris Exposition of 1889, the actual year of one of the expositions. (There was no exposition in 1883.) According to this source, the ocean trip was difficult, and the Indians got seasick during the voyage. Julius and his Indian companions reportedly remained in France for nearly a year.

If Julius had traveled abroad in 1883, it would have historical importance. Carolyn Foreman, a noted Indian historian, wrote that "Indians were carried abroad for the purpose of exploiting them to enrich white men of the U.S.," and noted, more importantly, that the idea started in Omaha in 1883 but she does not name the originator of the idea. For the next twenty-five years, a continuous stream of Indians crossed and re-crossed the Atlantic Ocean to Europe to entertain various heads of state. Buffalo Bill's "Wild West Show," with a cast of seventy-five Sioux, made many crossings to perform in England, France, Austria, Spain, Hungary, and Belgium—even the Vatican, but none of these crossings took place until 1887. Another flamboyant showman, Gordon W. Lillie, known as Pawnee Bill, toured Europe with a troop of Indians, but not until 1894.

Between 1866 and 1886, the Meyer brothers' business expanded rapidly, and after a series of moves, settled at Sixteenth and Farnam in 1887. Max and Adolph were partners in the jewelry and music operation while Max and Moritz formed the cigar partnership. Throughout this period Julius ran his "Indian Wigwam" while at the same time he maintained a close business relationship with his brothers.

At the height of its success at Sixteenth and Farnam, the Meyer firm, now doing business as Max Meyer and Bro. and Max Meyer and Co., was one of the largest retail outlets of its kind in the West. The cigar store had a twenty-five-foot frontage on Farnam and ran 132 feet in depth. Above the cigar store on the second floor, the brothers had located their wholesale jewelry and watchmaking operation. The third floor was used mainly to store musical instruments.

A shopper entering the store on Sixteenth Street instead of on Farnam would come upon the jewelry and music store, crammed in every corner with jewelry, diamonds, watches, silverware, optical goods, musical merchandise, books, and small instruments. The piano sales room, which was located on the second floor, was furnished very grandly, like the living room of a wealthy person. The basement held stocks of tobacco, together with a jewelry manufacturing operation.

The firm had seventy-five employees, not including the twelve traveling salesmen who sold pianos, cigars, and jewelry in Iowa, Nebraska, Colorado, Utah, Kansas, Wyoming, and the Dakotas.

Unfortunately, within a few years the Meyer brothers' success as the kingpins of merchandising came to an end. The big store at Sixteenth and Farnam was destroyed in a fire in 1889. Although the brothers tried to rebuild their business at another location, it was too late. They could not rebuild their former success, and the business eventually failed in the depression of 1893.

Max, the leader of the Meyer clan, had been one of the most powerful men in Nebraska. He was an organizer of the Omaha Commercial Club, which was the forerunner of the Chamber of Commerce. He served four terms as president of the Omaha Board of Trade, and had been a charter member. In addition, he was a principal of the Omaha Savings Bank, the first bank of its kind in Omaha. Max left Omaha after the failure of the store and spent his remaining years in New York.

Adolph became an insurance salesman and continued in this work after he had moved to Chicago. He died suddenly in that city a short time after settling there.

Moritz opened his cigar store, and Julius closed his "Indian Wigwam" forever. It is probable that Julius had been associated with his brother Adolph in the insurance business until Adolph left Omaha.

The news of Julius's death was a front page story in the Omaha newspapers. In one account, the first paragraph read:

> Lying beside a bench in Hanscom Park, a bullet hole in his left temple and another in his left breast, a revolver clenched in his left hand, the body of Julius Meyer, president of the Metropolitan Club and a resident of Omaha for over forty years, was found at 11:50 Monday forenoon...

The article went on to point out that both his housekeeper and Mr. Adler, from whom he leased his rooms, could give no reason why he would have wanted to kill himself. Both asserted that Julius was in good spirits and financially well-off. His brother, Moritz, also was unable to explain the suicide. "He had been sick," Moritz was quoted as saying, "but was recovering. As far as I know, his financial condition was all right."

The obituary went on to point out that "in making away with himself, he had evidently shot himself first in the temple and then turned the gun against his breast."

On the one hand, Julius Meyer was a basic, practical-minded merchant, fearless enough to live among the Indians and trade with them. But there was another side of his character. He was also like a butterfly in a prairie boom town—a man of culture, who loved music and enjoyed entertaining. The true nature of his intentions when he left Moritz's store on that spring morning in 1909 will doubtless forever be buried in the past. Was he just another aging man, at peace with himself, out for a morning stroll, puffing on one of his brother's fine cigars? Or was some dark and destructive mission moving him toward Hanscom Park?

The people of Omaha could never explain the mystery of his death, and there is no record of any further investigation beyond the final conclusion that his death was a suicide. In fact, the suicide ruling was made almost immediately after the body was discovered.

The most puzzling fact led to an unanswered question: How could Julius have shot himself in the temple without killing himself as a result of that single shot? And if that shot had not killed him at once, why did he turn the gun against his breast instead of discharging it once more into his temple?

Julius's passion for posing for photographs with the Indians may provide an important clue to the mystery. In the photograph in which Julius is seen sitting around a campfire holding a peace pipe and surrounded by six Indian warriors, Julius grips the peace pipe in his right hand. In still another photograph, Julius, wearing a coonskin cap and Indian buckskin breeches, has a knife and scabbard strapped to his right hip. These photos could conceivably prove that Julius was right-handed. It does not seem likely that a man who would use a knife, if he had to, with his right hand would hold a gun with his left hand to shoot himself.

Why would Uncle Julius, a happy, lifelong bachelor, stroll over to Hanscom Park, roughly a two-mile walk from his apartment on Farnam Street, to commit suicide when the deed could have been accomplished in his own apartment? Why would he have cheerfully stopped at his brother's store for a cigar, then wave to him as he was on his way? And, most perplexing of all, if he had met with foul play, who would want to do away with that beloved little showman, "Box-Ka-Re-Sha-Hash-Ta-Ka"? And for what reason? Even if he had an unsuspected enemy, why would he have waited so many years, when Uncle Julius was getting old, to do away with him?

Julius's funeral services were private, held in the home of his sister, Mrs. Herman Rehfeld. A follow-up newspaper story noted that many letters and flowers were received at the Rehfeld home. All of the organizations of which Julius was a member—the Musicians Union, the Knights of Pythias, the Metropolitan Club and the Douglas County Pioneers—asked to attend the ceremony. The family said no because of the circumstances surrounding his death.

Rabbi Frederick Cohn delivered a short eulogy, then "Box-Ka-Re-Sha-Hash-Ta-Ka" was carted off to Pleasant Hill cemetery on his way to do some trading with the greatest Chief of them all.

THE UNUSUAL CASE OF DON SOLOMONO

The village of the Acoma Indians of New Mexico is high on a mesa (plateau), thirteen miles south of Interstate Highway 40 on State Route 13, about sixty miles west of Albuquerque. This part of the state is now seven thousand feet above the sea, but the land is very flat and the mountains in the distance form a border around what had been a sea. This flat land is interrupted only by stunning blue-brown mesas, or table-lands, which rise sharply from the high desert. Here and there one can see the twisted shapes of rock formations. They call the Acoma pueblo Sky City because it rises 360 feet above the desert under the big New Mexico sky. To the Indians, however, who have lived there for centuries and still speak the Queresan language, the city high on the rock is called by its Indian nickname, Ako—in Queresan, "a place that always was." In fact, today it is the oldest continuously-settled community in the United States, and some archaeologists say it dates from before the birth of Christ.

Although the main language of the Indians is Queresan, most also speak English, while only a few of the older people

still speak Spanish. The houses of the pueblo were similarly constructed; all were private and connected, with the top floor used as the living room, the middle floor for sleeping, and the ground floor for storage. To get into the house, the Indians used an outside ladder which led directly to the balcony of the second floor.

Three miles north of Acoma, rising sharply higher and steeper than Sky City, is Katzimo, the Enchanted Mesa. Legend tell us that Katzimo was once inhabited, but one day a severe storm destroyed the rock trail leading to the settlement on top. Since they were unable to go down to the valley for food, the natives eventually died of hunger. No one really knows whether anyone had ever lived on Katzimo, but, as the story goes, "No one ever climbs that mesa, for the pathway down will vanish behind them."

For the past four hundred years the Indians of Acoma have lived under the domination of three different nations—Spain, Mexico, and the United States. During all this time, there has been a continuing and difficult problem because of the lands originally granted to the various New Mexico pueblos by the Spaniards. The troubled years resulted in countless disputes between the Indians and the nations in power, between Indians and white settlers, and among various Indian groups themselves. From 1684, when the Spaniards first made their land grants to the Indians until this very day, the disagreements remain unsettled. That is why the telling of any story acted out in the history of New Mexico, no matter how unimportant it may seem, will in some way have its beginning in the ongoing dispute over land ownership. And it is too with the strange case of Solomon Bibo.

The first historical reference to Acoma came in 1539. Fray Marcos de Niza, a priest returning from a visit to New Mexico, told of a settlement on the mesa and referred to it as a Kingdom of Hacus (the native name for their tribe, Acoma being a Spanish version). Hearing of the discovery, Francisco Coronado, the Spanish explorer, sent Captain Hernando Alvarado to explore further. The following year, Alvarado reached the pueblo, describing it as "a very strange place built upon a solid rock."

Alvarado's men were greeted by the Indians and made welcome, after they had successfully climbed the rock trail to the top of the mesa. They were presented with gifts of food, for there was nothing threatening in the behavior of Alvarado's men. It was merely a routine exploration, and so the Indians were friendly to their visitors. At this time, about 200 lived in the pueblo. Later Spanish expeditions came there in 1581 and 1582, but nothing changed until 1598, when Spain believed it was necessary to force the Indians to submit to Spanish rule. The following year, Vincente de Zaldivar and a force of seventy men cautiously scaled the rock trail to the top of the mesa, and, after a fierce struggle, managed to overpower the natives and take command of the village even though they were greatly outnumbered.

In 1629, a gentle Franciscan monk, Fray Juan Ramirez, arrived at the pueblo. He had been forewarned that the Indians were bitterly hostile toward white men, but the fearless Ramirez won them over. He also taught them to read and write, led them into Christianity, and built the mission San Estevan. Somehow, after these gentle inroads, it became possible for Christianity to live side by side with the Indians' tribal practices until the Spanish, who were ardent Catholics, insisted on only their own religion. In 1680, the Spaniards tried to wipe out the Indians' religious practices. The Indians revolted and overthrew the Spaniards.

After the pueblo revolt, Acoma remained independent until the Spanish reconquered it in 1692. Spanish domination continued for the next 130 years until the signing of the treaty of Cordova in 1821, when New Spain became New Mexico, part of the Mexican nation.

As subjects of the Spanish king, the Indians had all the privileges of any Spaniard. They were entitled to their own lands and to full protection under church and civil law. Non-Indians were strictly forbidden to live on Indian property and could not even stop there for a night if other facilities were available. No one could violate the Indians' right to their own land, and they, in turn, were forbidden to live in another village. Moreover, they were not allowed to buy or sell their property without the approval of the Spanish authorities. All that Spain asked in return from the Indians was that they become Christians, marry under Christian law, and that they learn to speak Spanish.

None of the Spanish rules and privileges regarding the Indians was as important as the Indian rights to all streams and rivers (as well as other water) which crossed or bordered their lands. This regulation, to this very day, is the reason for the three-way dispute among the pueblo Indians, the descendants of the Spanish settlers, and New Mexico's growing wealthy Anglo (English-speaking) population.

On September 16, 1821, Mexico won her independence from Spain, but the Mexicans were bound by treaty to uphold

Jewish Heroes of the Wild West

the Spanish laws regarding Indian land and water policy. Although the Indians were technically wards of the government under Spanish rule, the Mexicans nevertheless gave them the title of citizens, and as citizens, they could sell, trade, or change their land grants, something they had been prevented from doing under Spanish rule.

Spanish law stated that non-Indians could not get control of pueblo lands. In reality, this law was not enforced because Mexican administrators and officials falsified titles to lands granted by Spain to the Indians. By doing so they were able to control pueblo lands without the Indians' knowledge. In addition, white squatters invaded the Indians' lands, and without protection the Indians saw the lands to which they were entitled dwindle away.

In 1846, the United States acquired New Mexico by purchasing it from Mexico, and this event had confusing results for the pueblos. One of those results was that anyone, including Solomon Bibo (about whose involvement with Indians lands we shall soon learn) could make deals with the Indians which could include their land, and some of these arrangements were unfair.

In 1846, the pueblo Indians automatically became full-fledged American citizens. Immediately, the government of the United States was faced with two problems for which it would seek solutions for a long time. One problem was how to deal with the loss of Indian lands to non-Indians; the other was how to justify the restraints the United States wanted to impose on the Indians without depriving them of their rights as citizens, rights they were given in the Treaty of Guadalupe-Hidalgo in 1848.

In section six of that treaty, the United States had to recognize the rights of Mexican citizens with respect to their property and other civil matters. Because the Mexicans had declared the Indians citizens when New Spain became New Mexico in 1821, the United States was now forced to give the Indians the same status. As a result, the position of the pueblo Indians became vastly different from that of other Indian groups living elsewhere on western reservations. The United States policy toward various Indian tribes was now in conflict because, previously, Indians had only been considered savages who needed to be controlled, not citizens with property rights.

In 1876, nearly thirty years after the Treaty of Guadalupe-Hidalgo, the Supreme Court strengthened the provisions of the treaty. It stated that the pueblo Indians were not Indians at all, and therefore the laws which applied to other Indians elsewhere did not apply to them. For that reason, they had complete title to their lands and could do anything they wished with them. In addition, the pueblos were assured that their land grants under Spain would be recognized, and for this reason the Office of Surveyor General was established in 1854 to investigate land ownership claims and decide whether they were valid. It was necessary to define the boundaries of the Indians' holdings, once and for all.

When a survey of Acoma lands was finally taken in 1858, the Indians could offer little proof of their original boundaries, since they had no maps or stakes before the arrival of the first explorers. Even though additional surveys were made in 1876 and 1877, the outcome for their claims was unfavorable. In 1877, President Rutherford B. Hayes agreed with the survey of 1858 and Acoma received its share of 94,196 acres, which was far less than the residents believed themselves entitled to.

****

On a cold, windy morning in May, 1885, a wedding took place in the village of the Acoma Indians. The entire village came to the ceremony, crowding into the old church, with its ten-foot thick adobe (hard-baked bricks of mud) walls which reached over sixty feet high. The ceiling was supported by heavy beams. The church dated from the seventeenth century

Jewish Heroes of the Wild West

and was named for Saint Estevan, the first martyr and patron saint of the Acoma Indians. During Indian revolts of 1680, the old church had served as a fortress for the tribe when their village was besieged.

The bride was a young Indian girl named Juana Valle, the granddaughter of the governor of the pueblo, which is the Spanish word both for town and people. Juana spoke no English, only Spanish and Queresan, the native tongue of the tribe. The groom was a small slightly plump man in his middle thirties. This, then, was Solomon Bibo, who had come from a town called Brakel in Germany. His father, Isaac Bibo, was a cantor.

The wedding was strange in many ways. Even though the Indians had become Catholics in 1628 with the arrival of the first missionaries, they kept many of their ancient tribal beliefs and customs. Solomon Bibo, on the other hand, was a Jew who lived among the Indians. On this day, although he was being married in a Catholic church to a Catholic woman against his own religious tradition, he nevertheless held on to his Jewish heritage.

The local Indians disliked the white men intensely because so much of Indian land. But Solomon Bibo had a different place in their hearts. The Indians had only love for him as he stood with his bride in the thick red-brown dust of the old church floor.

In April, 1884, a year before his marriage to Juana, the Acoma tribe leased its entire 94,196 acres to Solomon Bibo. Nothing in life was as important to the tribe as its land, yet for a period of thirty years the Indians signed away their rights to Bibo, who now held the full land title granted to them in 1877.

The lease called for Bibo to pay the tribe $300 per year for the first ten years; $400 for the second ten years; and $500 per year for the remaining ten years—in all, $12,000 for the full thirty years. Bibo in return would be responsible for protecting the Indians' cattle and for keeping squatters (people who settle in places to which they have no rights) off the land. However, under the terms of the lease, Bibo had both mining and water rights, and would pay the Indians ten cents per ton for each ton of coal taken from the land. Bibo also had the right to give the lease to anyone he chose during the life of the agreement.

The Spanish-speaking Indians called Bibo "Don Solomono." In doing so, they showed him great respect, for in Spanish the title "don" is like the English "sir." He had been in the New Mexico Territory for more than seventeen years, and even though his English was poor, he spoke fluent Queresan and Spanish. It was not easy for a white European man to learn the Indians' language, but he was very friendly as a trader with them and, because he had spent many years at the pueblo, his quick mind helped him to learn.

Bibo was born on August 29, 1853, in Prussia (an eastern province of Germany in which the capital city of the country, Berlin, is located). There were eleven children of Blumchen Rosenstein Bibo and her husband, Isaac and Solomon was the sixth born child. He immigrated to America in 1869, when he was sixteen. He left his homeland for very common reasons at that time—anti-Semitism was becoming stronger in Germany, and there was the promise of greater economic opportunity in America. Besides these two important motivations, he had heard from his grandfather, Lucas Rosenstein, vivid recollections accumulated when Lucas had come to America to escape being drafted into Napoleon's

Jewish Heroes of the Wild West

army. Lucas had stayed twelve years in America, but returned to his native land to marry his childhood sweetheart. Solomon and his brothers were deeply affected by their grandfather's tales of the New World.

Nathan and Simon, the first two Bibo brothers to come to America, are believed to have spent only a very little time in the east when they arrived in 1866. As adventuresome young men, they  headed straight for New Mexico, where they worked for a time for the Spiegelberg Brothers business in Santa Fe, which at that time was a center of developing commerce. (The Spiegelbergs were part of a German-Jewish network which helped newly-arrived fellow-countrymen, young immigrants, to find work.) However, because Nathan and Simon wanted no part of the dry goods business as a permanent way of making a living, they pushed farther west toward Albuquerque. Eventually, they opened a trading post at the small village of Ceboletta, New Mexico, and started trading with the Navajos. Solomon arrived three years later, but he spent more time on the eastern seaboard than his brothers because he wanted to become more fluent in English. After a time he moved westward and joined his brothers as a partner in their trading post at Ceboletta.

It is known that in about 1871 Simon was a licensed trader at the Laguna pueblo, near Acoma. Both Nathan and Simon were engaged in bidding on the produce requirements for Fort Wingate and Fort Defiance, with the Indians as their main source of supply. All three brothers were friends and supporters of the Indians and they became closely involved in the Indians' land boundary problems.

Solomon arrived at Acoma in 1882 and set up his trading post near the mission, but from the beginning he had problems getting a license. It is believed that because he supported an unpopular position, that of securing more land for the Indians, he found himself in difficulties with local politicians. He was also considered a trouble-maker by the Mexicans, who believed that the Indians were trying to dispossess them from their property in an effort to reclaim their original tribal lands. He was also called "un rico Israelito" (a rich Jew). In order to secure his trader's license, he had to get help from the Spiegelbergs, who had great influence in political matters about territory. They were also welcome in the drawing-rooms of influential people of Santa Fe, a privilege not shared by many Jews.

Two months after Bibo had made his own agreement with the Acoma Indians, Pedro Sanchez, the Indian agent from Santa Fe, found out about it and on June 14, 1884 wrote an angry letter to Hiram Price, the Commissioner of Indian Affairs. He told Price that Bibo had taken advantage of the Indians because of their ignorance. Sanchez went on to say that Valle's mark on the lease expressed only his own will, not necessarily that of all his people.

Price's response to Sanchez was that his office would not give its approval to Bibo's action. It seemed that both Sanchez and Price had made up their minds that Bibo had cheated the Acoma, and they wished to determine if the agreement indeed represented the will of the people.

Sanchez met with Valle, the governor, and handed him a document to sign with his mark. This document stated that Bibo had misled Valle to believe that the lease was only for three, not thirty, years. With this in his pocket, Sanchez met with 60 members of the tribe and asked if they had consented to the original agreement. All quickly denied that they had given their consent, Martin Valle included. Sanchez now had what he needed to have Bibo's trading license suspended. But Bibo insisted that the lease was legally binding and that he had no intention of setting it aside. At that point, when Price found out what was going on, he ordered Sanchez to revoke Bibo's license to trade.

The Indians begged the commissioner to permit Bibo to continue trading, for Bibo's love and friendship was so important to them that they produced 100 signatures in his behalf.

Because Solomon's brother Simon believed earnestly that no one could prevent Solomon from trading with the Indians as long as they wanted him, he had the Indians prepare the petition with the 100 signatures. He wrote of his brother Solomon, "His intentions with the Indians are of the best nature and beneficial to them—because the men, women and children love him as they would love a father and he is in the same manner attached to them."

What Bibo's foes did not know was that the Acoma had been approached by two traders, brothers named Marmon, who attempted to lease the land from the Acoma, offering them one cow a year for ten years. In exchange, the Indians, having full trust in Bibo, came to him with this outrageous proposal, and he offered to lease the land himself in order to protect them from dishonest traders.

Simon told the whole story to General Whittlesey, a member of the Board of Indian Commissioners, who, fortunately, was impressed with the apparent honesty of Bibo's action. The General notified Price that he believed Bibo was a true friend of the Indians and that suspending his license was not in the best interests of the tribe.

Joseph Bell, the United States attorney, concluded in 1888, four years after the government sued Bibo for defrauding the Indians of their land, that the government had no case. Not wanting to turn their backs on their beloved friend, the Acoma did not want to support the complaint. The charges were dropped, and Pedro Sanchez, the government's Indian agent, was replaced. The new agent, W. D. Williams, sent a letter to the pueblo in October, 1888. He wrote:

> To the people of the pueblo of Acoma, having confidence in the ability, integrity and fidelity of Solomon

Bibo, and by virtue of the authority vested in me as Indian Agent by the United States, I hereby appoint Solomon Bibo governor of said pueblo.

> (Signed) W. D. Williams
> U.S. Indian Agent

Thus, Solomon Bibo, a Jewish immigrant, who four years earlier had been charged with defrauding the Indians of their land, was now governor of the pueblo, not just the only Jew but also the only white man in the history of Acoma to hold that title, a title which means "chief" to members of the tribe.

The career of Solomon Bibo will probably always remain somewhat mysterious. Certainly he had deep and sincere feelings for the Indians, living with them, learning their language, marrying into the tribe even against his own religious principles. In addition to working hard to help with their land disputes, he also fought to improve the quality of their education by arranging for the admission of some of them to the Carlisle Indian School, including his own wife, Juana. Nothing can detract from the heartfelt goodness of this man. Rabbi Floyd Fierman, a historian who wrote about Jews in the old West, concluded that the Indians, dating back to their rule under the Spaniards, were in constant fear that they might have their land taken away from them, and as a result placed their trust in Bibo by giving him the long lease he arranged for. In this way, he could save them from others who would take advantage of them.

At this time in our history, we do know that government policy regarding native Americans has frequently been insensitive and unfair. Through no fault of their own, the Indians were fair game for all sorts of con men along the Santa Fe trail. While some other tribes received special protections on reservations, the pueblo Indians eventually became citizens with no special government protection. In 1913, the Supreme Court overturned the ruling which made them citizens, declaring them to be wards of the government. In its decision, the Court held that:

> The people of the pueblos, although sedentary rather than nomadic in their inclinations and disposed to peace and industry, are nevertheless Indians in race, customs, and domestic government...adhering to primitive modes of life, largely influenced by superstition and fetishism...They are essentially a simple, uninformed and inferior people.

(No responsible citizen today, let alone a court of law, would dream of writing such a decision! We freely acknowledge the injustices of the past and are helping young people to shape new and healthy attitudes about all the different groups in our country who play such a vital role in all its affairs and activities. We have come a long way from believing that because their way of life is different, Indians are "uninformed and inferior.")

Solomon and Juana and their family moved to San Francisco in 1898. He invested in real estate and was president of Bibo, Newman and Ikenberg, a fancy food store located at the corner of Polk and California streets. Sadly, the business was destroyed in the earthquake of 1906. It is interesting to note that the move to California was made chiefly because Solomon Bibo wanted his children to receive a Jewish education.

There were six Bibo children, four daughters and two sons. The eldest boy, LeRoy, attained bar mitzvah at San Francisco's Ohabai Shalome (the Bush Street Synagogue). The younger son, Carl, attended religious school at Temple Emanuel. Juana Bibo also observed the Jewish faith.

Loved by the Indians as few white men ever were, Don Solomono died in San Francisco in 1934 at eighty-one. LeRoy and Carl, his two sons, said Kaddish for their father at Congregation Shearith Israel. Juana Bibo died seven years later, in 1941. The Jewish Acoma chief and his princess are buried in Colma, California, at the Home of Peace Mausoleum.

Jewish Heroes of the Wild West

Their friend, historian-archaeologist Charles Lummis, dedicated one of his books to Solomon and Juana. The surviving son, Carl Bibo, received a copy of the dedication. It read:

> To Sol and Juana Bibo, whom I have known and loved for forty years, since the dear old days in New Mexico, when they were beginning that married life which has been, to this day, so beautiful an example and so rare an inspiration. Dona Juana, of the oldest aristocracy in this country, worthy daughter of the First Americans, whose noble grandfather first told me the story of the Enchanted Mesa, is a much finer type than the storied Pocahontas, and of better blood. Don Solomon has left his mark all across New Mexico as one of the wisest, shrewdest, high-minded, most just and most generous of men that ever dealt with the natives of the Southwest. I write here of many things that they have shared, and I hope this book may bring back to them as many gentle memories as it does to me.

On the typed copy of that dedication, the word "shrewdest," which has a negative tone, had been crossed out in ink!

Historians have often given the impression that the Indians were oppressed under the Spaniards. Actually, the conquerors were far more humane than they were given credit for. Charles F. Lummis, pointed out that there were seventy-six pueblos at the time of Spain's conquest of the Indians, but the Spaniards persuaded them to concentrate into far fewer pueblos. Larger communities, they pointed out, were less likely to be attacked by warring neighbors. The newly-populated pueblos became the Spanish land-grants that are still being disputed today. In 1893, Lummis described the effects of Spanish rule on the Indians:

> The most important effect of the coming of Spain was to make the pueblo from a sedentary to a fixed Indian...To each of his communities was given a generous grant of land, and upon that grant he must stay. Thenceforth there were no town migrations, and the living pueblos are essentially where they were when Plymouth Rock came into history...With greater fixity of abode he has still further increased the distance between himself and the nomad. His perceptions have grown less acute than those of the hunted hunter—though still far ahead of the Caucasian—but he has reflected more, acquired more, and preserved more. His traditions have accumulated to a huge mass; his laws are well-formulated; his internal religion has been bewilderingly complex. It is fortunate for archaeology that the Spaniard was his brother's keeper. Had the pueblo enjoyed sixteenth century acquaintance with the Saxons, we should be limited now to unearthing and articulating his bones.

It has been well over a century since Solomon Bibo first came to the pueblo. What he saw when he first arrived was almost the same as what Alvarado had seen in 1540, except for the mission of San Estevan and the adjoining cemetery. The adobe houses were almost exactly the same. Built on the surface of the rock, they were three stories high and lined up in parallel rows, running east and facing south.

Today, as in the past, Acoma land is used for grazing, but farming is the chief occupation, with wheat, beans, corn, alfalfa, and chili being the main products. The Acoma community has strongly resisted moving into the twentieth century, and the older members of the tribe have tried to keep the pueblo much the same as it was in former centuries in order to hold their power. The cacique (chief), the medicine man, the war chief, and the governor, part of the same tribal organization of the past, still remain in control. The Queresan language is still spoken, and as late as the 1930's, very few of the older people had ventured more than a few miles from the reservation. About ninety-nine percent of the tribe still continues to reside on Acoma lands.

The old village on the mesa is now only a symbolic home for the tribe, and no longer the main village. The Indians live mostly in the valley surrounding the mesa, but a few keep their homes in the old village during the warmer months of the year. The income of the Indians remains pitifully low, and those who are not farmers have various jobs off the reservation. Modern facilities such as gas stations, restaurants, and motels are not found on the reservation, and the Indians take care of their shopping needs in small Mexican-American communities nearby.

Today the reservation consists of 245,672 acres in contrast to the 94,196 acres of the original Spanish land grant recorded by the United States in 1877. The present lands were set aside by Congress in March, 1928, after recognizing the pueblo's need for more pasture land to feed their animals. The Acoma reservation is home for one of the nineteen different pueblo tribes in New Mexico and is composed of three parts - Acoma, the old village on top of the mesa; Acomita, a farm community in the north valley of the reservation; and McCarty's, located on the reservation's north gap, along the right of way of the Atchison, Topeka, and Santa Fe railroad.

Through most of the nineteenth century, the Laguna and the Acoma pueblos were constantly fighting over their boundaries, but today they live in peace. Naturally, whenever there was a dispute, Bibo sided with the Acoma, thus angering the Laguna, the white traders doing business with them, and the Mexicans, who took whichever side was best for them. Solomon Bibo had consistently helped his friends, the Acoma Indians, with their petitions to increase their boundaries, and he lived long enough to see his hopes for them fulfilled.